Becoming A Confident Lady of Purpose

Introducing the

7 PRINCIPLES of SELF within OUR...

I~N~N~E~R BEAUTY

CJ Fortson

CJF

PUBLISHING

Becoming A Confident Lady of Purpose
Introducing 7 Principles of Self Within our I~N~N~E~R Beauty
© 2020 by CJ Fortson

Printed in the United States of America.
ISBN-13: 978-1-7353705-5-2

Icons made by Eucalyp, Smashicons, Smalllikeart, dDara and Freepil from positive.flaticon.com

Cover photo by CJ Fortson

CJF Publishing
Granbury, Texas
innerbeautyconfidence@outlook.com

We Would Like the World to Know We Are...

Extraordinary Ladies

Exploring Our Image

Educating Our Minds

Enriching Our Hearts

Encouraging Our Souls

Expanding Our Self-Worth

"By the grace of GOD, I am what I am." 1 Corinthians 15:10

The Confident Lady of Purpose Ministries

TABLE OF CONTENTS

ACKNOWLEDGMENTS

**I dedicate this book to every Lady who reads it and
takes the messages to Heart.**

I want to say a huge THANK YOU to my 'GOD-GIFT'–
my husband, David, for if it had not been for his love and
uplifting encouragements through the years, I wouldn't be at
this spectacular place in my life! David, you mean more to me
than I could ever write into words. I thank GOD for bringing
you into my life in 2002, it's been the greatest journey of my
lifetime! Thanks for your kind and patient love and walking
beside me and holding me up when I needed it throughout
this great 'Dream Becoming A Reality' for me.

Also, thanks to my two grown sons, Shain and Christopher,
for their encouragements throughout this writing process. I
love you both beyond the stars in the sky! GOD carried the
three of us through many, many rough times in your young
lives. The two of you were always my reason to stand as strong
as I could during those times and push onward.

I have to give another huge Thank You to two very special friends of mine for taking me into their home in 1996, after my former husband's death and helping me get back on my feet, while figuring out my new life. I could never repay you for the love, support and compassion you gave me throughout that emotional time and for the rough years that came afterwards! Don and Cray Pickering and my girls, I love you all so deeply and you will always hold a special place in my life and in my heart forever and ever!

Thank you to Tracy and Eric Sullivan, for if GOD had not placed you two in our lives, this book publication may not have happened. Thank you, Tracy, for being a great support throughout my writing process, and for recommending Publify Consulting. A Heartfelt THANK YOU to Mr. Lopez (Publisher), Nicole Donoho (Editor) for being such a tremendous help to me and for your encouragements all through the editing! Thank you to the Publify Publishing staff for all your work throughout this publication process.

Special Thanks as well to the following people for the part you have played in helping me throughout the writing of this book and covering me with prayers, encouragements and meals. Those who helped with pre-editing before going to Publify Publishing included Cray Pickering, JoAnn Adkins and Sarah Frink. Also, Thank You for the prayers, encouragements, and support from the... 'Women of Wisdom Focus Group', you Ladies were an uplifting group. And, Thank You to ALL of my 'Praying and Encouraging Family and Friends.' I love you all!

PERSONAL NOTE FROM CJ

Hello beautiful confident Ladies of purpose! Throughout this book you will notice I have capitalized the letter 'L' in the word... Lady. There is a special reason I have chosen to do this! I want every Lady who reads this book to feel **"fearfully and wonderfully made with strength and dignity."** as **Psalms 139:14** & **Proverbs 31:25** states.

Why? Because, in this day and age we seem to forget that we are very special to GOD, and by honoring you with a capital letter 'L' I'm honoring GOD for our creation as Loving, Caring, Ladies!!! You'll notice, too, I capitalized ALL the letters when referencing our Heavenly FATHER, GOD, SAVIOR, JESUS, HE or HIM.

This book has been compiled from files of papers and notebooks I've written and taught over the years, as a Bible Study, named, "HAVING the CONFIDENCE WALK & POSTURE IN CHRIST" - 'THE I~N~N~E~R BEAUTY FORMULA'. I have now changed the word formula into RECIPE.

I felt the LORD calling me to use this time during the 2020 Coronavirus shutdown to finish this book. As all would agree, I'm sure, we're not liking the 'locked-away-quarantine-feeling of 2020' that we're having to experience at the moment, but it has benefited me with lots of solitude time to finish the "BECOMING A CONFIDENT LADY of PURPOSE" Book!

The question I'll start off with... Is this not where so many of us have placed much of our personal Self-Respect, Self-Love, Self-Esteem, Self-Motivation, Self-Confidence, and Self-Worth? 'Locked Away ... in Isolation' to the point we do not see ourselves having strong Principles within our I~N~N~E~R SELF? There are also some Ladies, like the younger me, who wore the invisible suffocating 'mask,' which keeps us from voicing who we really are or would love to become! So, Ladies, I truly hope you will take the time to read through this book, page-by-page, at least once, pray, and allow God to speak to you. I pray this book will touch you and give you a totally new life by strengthening your I~N~N~E~R BEAUTY!

CJ Fortson

INTRODUCTION

This book is designed where it can be used in a
Bible Study group setting.

A 'Flashlight Version'
On What You Will See in This Book...

Some of the things you will be reading throughout this book
may not be actually what you want to hear. Some things may
be hard for you to apply into your own personal life, and
that's understandable. I totally can relate, because I had plenty
of uneasiness while writing a few parts of this book. As an
example, the things that GOD was revealing to me, while
writing about my own personal SELF that I didn't want to
accept or change. Yet, deep down I knew I needed to alter
many of my beliefs, thoughts, and over all my Mind-and
Heart-set! As I've stated, much of the contents of this book
has been taken out of manuscripts I wrote for my Ladies Bible
classes beginning in 2004.

What are your "ITs"? Are there things you believe about yourself that need changing? Are you willing to pray and ask GOD to reveal them to you, if you don't already know? Are you ready to 'let the negatives go' and let GOD erase the burden you may be carrying around with you out of your Mind and Heart? Or, maybe you're in need of a boost, or renewal, in your positive "ITs". Here's where you may need to ask GOD for a renewal in your Mind-and-Heart-Set! Wait a minute, don't throw this book down yet! There is a reason you picked it up to begin with! One or more of the reasonings listed below could be why:

- GOD has had it in HIS plan all along for you to be holding and reading this book.
- You may have been wanting to fill a void in your life, and you feel something you'll read in the book just might be the answer, and it very well may.
- You see something in the I~N~N~E~R BEAUTY RECIPE that is missing in your Journey-Walk, that you so desire to have in your Belief-System, in order to take your Self-Worth to a much higher level.

I know for some, this book is going to be hard to take in, maybe not because of its contents, but because of the messages that speaks to you personally. But, when the message on the pages begin to speak into your soul, keep reading and praying because the outcome will be magnificent!

Ladies, it's not my aim to try and change your beliefs, my purpose is to share the message GOD has given me to share with you, the rest is between you and our LORD and SAVIOR.

One more point I'd like to make: You will be reading shortly about some of my dreadful Journey-Walks and you may even ask why I'm sharing these terrible moments. First of all, there are things in my past I hate talking about, and some of those times are written within the pages of this book. But, if I can help one Lady to see hope, forgiveness and a new life by reading my story, that's the reason why GOD had me write about my past.

Never forget, if you've gone through darkness in your life and have found a new, changed, and brighter life, chances are, someone near you, or someone who hears or reads your testimony, will receive the message that they too can have hope and promise of a new and blessed life!

This is why we should never judge a Lady by her 'cover-up', because we don't know the deep, dark valleys she's had to endure in her lifetime that she never shares with others. She's learned how to... 'cover-up' her past.

OUR JOURNEYS

Journey-Walks are in reference to us walking through LIFE

Journey-Crawls are the times we seem to be crawling through life, because of being beaten down or the heavy burdens we're forced to carry at the moment

Journey-Hallelujahs are the times in life we feel like shouting with joy because of the blessings that have been showered upon us!

MY PERSONAL JOURNEY-WALK STORY

I want to begin with sharing a little about my past personal Journey-Walks, Journey-Crawls and Journey-Hallelujahs so you may get an idea of some of the things I've endured throughout my lifetime. The bad along with the good; the tears and the humor; the homeless times and princess times; and the dark valleys along with the highest mountain peaks! In so many of my Journey-Walks you would have found me crawling not walking.

JOURNEY HALLELUJAHS

My first Journey-Hallelujahs would be when my two sons were born. The first time I held them in my arms. The times they would hug my neck with tight hugs. I still love those hugs, even if they are now grown men. They were, and still are, the joys of my life, and I thank GOD for both of them!

Another Journey-Hallelujah is the past 19 years that I've been married to my GOD-Gift, my husband, David. He is truly a GIFT from GOD to me! So many blessings that I can't count them all throughout these 19 adventurous years, and I'm looking forward to many, many more!

More Journey-Hallelujahs were the times I did runway modeling, starting at the age of 19. It all started at my hometown country club, where I modeled bridesmaid's dresses and evening gowns for bridal shows and Ladies Tea Parties. I did many fashion shows throughout the years. I modeled through modeling agencies like, Robert Spence Modeling Agency in Lubbock, TX. While modeling department store garments, I had my picture in newspapers, local town magazines, and department stores advertisements. I even had the great opportunity of modeling on the runway with Miss USA, 1988... more on that story later. When I retired from modeling, I began teaching young teenage girls the importance of social etiquette, dining protocol, and how to present themselves as poised, confident, beautiful young Ladies, while in public and private settings.

Last, but surely not least of my Journey-Hallelujahs is having a long-time dream becoming a reality in writing my first book! GOD-willing, this is the first of several books I would love to have published. It's already been a rejoiceful adventure.

Now, I'm going to share with you a fraction of the other side of my personal life and why I believe GOD called me into Ladies Ministry. Buckle up Ladies and hang on till the end, and please no judging, because the end is so much better than the beginning and the middle of my Journey Walk and Crawls! Those of you who know me now, know I'm no longer the person you're about to read about! PRAISE GOD!

JOURNEY-CRAWLS
A Horrible Suffocating Belief Bubble!!!

Growing up, and even throughout my young adult life, I was the person that everyone said wouldn't amount to anything. I'd always heard I was a loser and that I would be a failure in life. The sad thing about that was, I believed them and lived my life in a horrible suffocating belief bubble! I had a very hard time throughout my life believing I could ever be anything I dreamed I wanted to be. No confidence, so therefore no motivation to prove them wrong, until later in my life! I don't remember my parents being 'parents of encouragement' to their children.

Throughout my young life, I saw my mother abused, to the point police were called more than once and took my dad to jail. When I became a teenager, I was also physically and verbally abused over and over throughout my teenage years while living at home. Once, when I was a young teenager, I was beaten so badly that when I went to work at our small town's Dairy Queen, I couldn't work in the front, because my eyes were so swollen from crying. Worse than that, blood was seeping through the back of my white blouse due to the belt lashes all across my back. My boss called the sheriff's office. They came and picked me up, took me home and took my dad away. He returned several hours later. As far as everyone in the small town was concerned, my dad was an upstanding citizen, so a warning was acceptable punishment.

I was raised in a very strict Christian home and was in church every time the doors were opened, literally. I came to know JESUS as my personal SAVIOR at the age of 12. We were very poor, but my dad was a hard-working man as a janitor in our town's school district. He loved talking to everyone, sometimes for hours. My mother always said my father was a good man, his problem was his quick-anger issues. No one else ever saw nor experienced his anger except my mother, younger brother, and myself. Not sure if my older sister ever went through abuse, she was 15 years older than I was, and now is with the Lord in heaven.

❦

When I saw a chance to marry and get away from home, I did just that. I jumped right into marriage at the early age of 18, he was 22. I was 17 when we got engaged and would have gotten married right then, but my parents wouldn't sign consent papers. So, we had to wait a few months until I turned 18. Three days after my 18th birthday, I walked down the aisle having no idea what a loving marriage was supposed to be like. I never saw love presented nor taught in my parent's home, so consequently, never knew how to give love into a marriage at that young age. Therefore, the marriage wasn't the best while we were together.

By the end of the sixth month into the marriage, I was pregnant with our first child, Shain, which was a rejoicing time for this young mother-to-be!

We moved many times, from Texas to New Mexico, and spent a year in Scotland, which I loved. After moving back to America, we had our second child, Christopher, that added more joy into my heart and life! We continued moving from town to town, house to house, and lived in a travel trailer for more than a year, with two small boys, a dog and a talking and singing parrot! If you don't think that wasn't a lot of fun, you should have been there with me! All I can say to that is, thank goodness I was still very young and had lots of energy, patience and endurance!

Later in our marriage, I got my Real Estate license. For the very first time in my life that was the belief key I used to start believing I could do anything I set out to do, if I put my mind and heart into it, and dedicated the time it took to accomplish my goals. We were married for 11 years when I filed for divorce. However, the divorce process went on for almost a year. The lifelong blessings that came from that marriage was my two sons that I love dearly, and to this day I'm still very proud of them and what they have accomplished in life!

When I first left my parent's house, I put GOD on the back burner. I only turned to HIM when I was in trouble. However, I called on HIM a lot during that time of being single and raising two children, with very little to mostly no child-support from their their dad. Isn't it ironic how we find ourselves content to go it alone when things are going well in our lives, but recognize our need for our SAVIOR when times are hard?

A year after my divorce was finally final, I remarried a much older man, believing I had found a gem that I truly believed loved me. Turned out, I ended up living in a dark hell hole for a year and four months, being physically and verbally abused once again, but to a much higher, horrific level. I, for sure, was left with no hope of ever having Self-Respect, Self-Confidence and no Self-Esteem. Truthfully, I'd never heard of those phrases until later in life.

I was back to where I started as a teenager with no Self-Worth. I was in constant hope and prayer this second husband would change back to the man he pretended to be during our short dating period... kind, loving and pleasant to be around. He always acted like he was so proud he was dating a much younger and beautiful woman, who had a professional career in the Real Estate business. He was a closing agent with one of the top Real Estate Title companies in town and was highly respected.

What people didn't know about this man was, twice in that short marriage, he tried to kill me. The first time was by trying to suffocate me after he forced a cleaner's plastic bag over my head and holding it very tightly around my neck until he thought I had passed out or, maybe, had suffocated to death. I guess his thoughts were, there would be no reason to question my death because there'd be no other proof than I died of natural causes. He was just an evil man! To this day, I will not keep plastic clothing bags from the dry cleaners in my closets. Even though the marriage to this horrible man was in the early 1980s, I still have extreme problems with anything tightly across my nose and mouth, so one of the hardest things I've experienced during the COVID-19 pandemic is wearing a mask.

Then, another time, he held me down on the bed with his knees and tried to choke me to death when he got so angry when I asked if I could buy something for the house. I managed to free myself from his strong hands after I kneed him... you know where. I ran out of the house and drove into town to get away from him, because I knew he would be even angrier. I was left with bruises around my neck, for a week or more, so badly that I couldn't leave the house for fear someone would see them and ask what happened. Thank goodness my boys were not at the house at the time this happened.

His "I'm sorry" was no longer accepted as sincere from that point on, because of the abuse. After both of those attempts on my life, and others, like when he tried to run over me in the garage with his car, he would threaten me with even more evil if I told anyone! He had me so mentally beaten down that I couldn't function normally as a human being and for that I was also punished. I found myself isolating from all my friends and family.

I was only allowed so much food on my plate at mealtimes, and he would take away my plate when he thought I'd had enough to eat, because he didn't want me to gain an ounce. I was already under-weight, at the height of 5'11".

It's kind of ironic to think about now; he didn't want me to gain an ounce, but yet he'd pick a fight with any man who looked at me, while we were out in public together and that embarrassed me to no end. He actually caused a scene at a restaurant one day that brought the manager to the table. A guy had turned and watched me walk by his table, unbeknownst to me. My husband was behind me, saw the man, and he verbally attacked him, but the man wasn't going to take it. What an embarrassment! With everyone looking our way to see what all the commotion was about; I went to the very back of the restaurant to find a table out of sight from the gazing eyes of those in the room. Guess who ended up getting the blame for that man looking at me? You guessed it...me! I wouldn't even look in the direction of another man, much less make eye contact with one, for fear my husband would see it and the abuse would come upon me again.

As if the physical and verbal abuse, taking food away from me wasn't enough, he even went as far as choosing all my clothes. He would go to department stores, choose what he liked and that was what I had to wear.

I always had to ask permission if I wanted to go somewhere other than work. Since I was a Realtor, I took that time to do some of the things I wanted to do, until one day when I caught him writing down the mileage on my car. Apparently, he had been doing that all along. That was why he would ask me, every day, every detail of my day. He would call my office and ask if I was in the office. And, when they'd send the call back to me, he would hang up before, or when, he heard my voice. After finding him writing down my car mileage, that's when I realized why he was calling me at work and would hang up. This was back in the early '80s, before cellphones.

He took each of my commission checks, until I stopped telling him I had a closing. It wasn't long before I got to the point where I was receiving fewer and fewer commission checks, because I was in no shape to deal with people. This husband wouldn't even introduce me as his wife to people he knew. He just stood and talked to them, as if I wasn't anywhere nearby. And on and on the embarrassments went.

Looking back, I can see the extreme level of control that he held over me, but at the time it had become my normal. It was something I had accepted as part of my life. I was brainwashed!

Then, there was the time when I had to have immediate hysterectomy surgery and the doctor asked some strange questions. I had to answer why I was in the shape I was in at that time, which I won't reveal in this book. My husband took me to the hospital, checked me in that morning and said he'd see me later. Thankfully, my sister and best friend were there to support me. When he told my sister to call and let him know how the surgery went, because he was going to work.

Things did not go over well. Needless to say, he got his mind changed upon strong demands from both my sister and my best friend, along with the nurses and my doctor, with all of them telling him exactly how he was going to spend his morning! I heard about the disturbing fiasco he caused a couple of days later from everyone but him. I do remember him coming back into my room – while I was waiting to go back for surgery – when he sat down took off his shoes and threw one across the room. I didn't say a word, because I was already going under from the medication I had just received.

Believe it or not, an unbelievable thing happened, he actually took good care of me during my recovery, which was a shock to everyone. He even took off a week in order to be home for me. He waited on me and even had very nice conversations with me during that recovery time. He had returned back to the caring man he was while we were dating. I kept one eye on him at all times, though. I don't know what that doctor, and others, had said to him, but, it worked, for a short while, until I was able to take care of myself. Then, his nice and caring demeaner slowly disappeared, and soon was no longer seen!

My oldest son had chosen to go live with his dad, because he was tired of being around this man. My ex-husband, knowing what his sons were living in, filed for custody of both our boys and took me to court. That's another horrific story. My ex-husband got custody of my oldest son, but not my youngest.

That was a road I traveled all alone during the process. I was still trying to regain my strength from surgery. My present husband was in no way supportive of me. He even caused a scene in the halls of the courthouse, because I wanted him to come home with me after losing custody of my oldest son. He told me that was my problem, not his. Then he turned around and walked out of the courthouse to his car and went back to work! I had felt alone many times throughout that marriage, but nothing like at that time.

My attorney walked me to my car, trying his best to calm me down. He even called later that day to check on me. He was a friend to my husband and couldn't believe what he'd just witnessed. Even the people closest to him had no idea what kind of man he really was at all. In our community, he was viewed as a respectable suit and tie wearing man, so I doubt anyone would have believed the horrors I'd endured every day. I seriously feared this second husband enough that I never told a soul of exactly what all I endured in our one-year and four-month marriage, until later in my life. He never harmed my sons in any way, I saw to that. He never paid them any attention. But, I feared he was setting a horrible example in front of them.

Ladies, I allowed this man to take all hope away from me from ever becoming the Lady and wife I truly wanted to be. Not to mention, the Lady that GOD had planned for me to be, even before my birth! After the very first abuse, I should have packed our bags, took my boys, and got out of there! I know you're probably asking, "CJ, why did you continue to stay with him?" Remember, he took my commission checks, so I didn't have a penny to my name. He made sure of that. He never placed me on his checking or savings accounts. Aside from all that, I feared what he'd do to me if I had left.

I sincerely hope, whomever is reading this, if you're in a relationship with any of this sort of abuse you will seek help! There's plenty of rescue places nowadays that you can run to for help and safety.

The Bible tells us in **Ezra 9:8b... "...our GOD gives light to our eyes and a relief in our bondage."** Ladies, a Women's Shelter gives light and a relief in your bondage, so DO NOT hesitate to find one, if you're living in a dangerous relationship! Verse 9 goes on to say... **"For our GOD has not deserted you in your bondage. He has shown you kindness – He has granted you new life to rebuild and repair your ruins."** Ladies! stop endangering yourself and your children! Seek GOD, and seek shelter quickly!

A year and four months after our marriage ceremony, it ended with him passing away of a sudden heart attack early one morning. He had gotten up to get ready for work, took the dogs out and came back into the bedroom. I felt him sit down on the bed rather hard. I just thought he was trying to begin the day being an annoyance, just being himself. Then, a few seconds later, he fell backwards on the bed and made some strange sounds. By the time I raised up in bed and looked over where he was laying, it seemed like he was no longer breathing. I jumped up and felt his neck for a pulse but couldn't find one. I ran immediately and called the EMS. They pronounced him dead upon arrival. The autopsy showed it was a heart attack. I'll always believe that GOD took this man, before he took me out for good. That's how bad it had been. It was a long time, before I ever shared with anyone what I endured during that marriage. And, the only reason I'm sharing it now is... if anyone reading this book sees themselves in this same type of abuse, there's help out there for you.

My oldest son returned back to me and his younger brother immediately after the funeral, which was the best part of this whole mayhem!! We quickly moved out of this man's house and began putting our lives back together again. We looked forward to peaceful and better times, which we were finally able to experience. I recovered from the fear of abuse, but it was many years before I could let go of all the psychological scars this man had left within me. By GOD's grace and love for HIS daughter, I managed to get on my feet. I was on a quest, searching for inner peace, Confidence and Self-Worth, blessings I'd never experienced much of in my lifetime, up to that point. Thank goodness, by listening to motivational speakers I would hear when attending Realtors Training and Conferences, I began to build up my Self-Confidence. I finally had come to the realization that it first had to begin with believing in myself, which was, in itself, a Journey-of-Learning for me!

Being a Realtor before this marriage, I returned to a career where I could make my schedule around my two young sons. I also got my insurance license, to bring in a little more income. At first, I wanted to experience a side of life I'd never known before, like going to bars for happy hours and partying into the wee hours when my sons were with their dad on his weekends to have them. Yes, I had fun partying and it made me temporarily feel important and special having lots of attention from men. However, nothing was ever really at peace in my mind and Heart.

Still being very skinny, I went back to doing some runway modeling for department stores to help build my Self-Esteem, or so I chose to believe.

19

We Can't Change Our Past – However, GOD Can Change the Roads to Lead Us into A Better and Brighter Future... If We Would Only Allow HIM to do IT!!! - A CJism

Three years later, I remarried, but this time to a wonderful man who put me up on a pedestal and showed the world he truly loved me. I finally knew what love was all about! He wasn't perfect, but neither was I. Even though our 14 years of marriage wasn't always a joy ride, our bad times never lasted long. A few years into our marriage, my husband became a Christian and our marriage was the greatest we'd ever experienced. I had finally experienced what LOVE was all about! Overall, being married to Larry were the best and most fun years of my entire life, up until he passed away after a very short battle with pancreatic cancer in 1996.

I never understood why GOD took him away from me. Actually, I was very angry at GOD, for a short time for not healing my husband and taking him away from me. I was also angry at finding myself emotionally and spiritually broken, all alone, penniless, and homeless for a few months. This was when my amazing friends took me in to stay with them for three months until I could get my life straightened out and back on my feet to get my own place.

A few years went by, with just trying to stay alive, struggling with my I~N~N~E~R Self and worrying that my life was never going to get any better. Then I started going to church. And, one day, I finally got to the point in my life where I knew I needed to let GOD do what HE wanted to do in my life, instead of me doing what I wanted to do, which was mostly worrying. That's when my life changed!

Ladies, I did not share this part of my life with you for you to feel sorry for me, but so you can understand why I'm the person I am today – a healed, whole and strong-willed Lady.

Rock-bottom heartbreaks will teach us lessons that mountain tops never will! - A CJism

"By the grace of GOD, I am what I am (today)."
1 Corinthians 15:10

I may not totally be who I need to be. I know I'm not all I want to be as of yet. But, by GOD's GRACE, I've come a long way from who I used to be. And, I won't ever give up on becoming what I know I can be and what GOD has called me to be!
- A CJism

Ladies, take these QUOTES and BIBLE verses to heart and develop a daily prayer from them as you talk to GOD.

"Surely it was for my benefit that I suffered such anguish.

In YOUR love YOU kept me from the pit of destruction;

YOU have put all my sins behind YOUR back.

For the grave cannot praise YOU, death cannot sing YOUR praise;

those who go down to the pit cannot hope for YOUR faithfulness.

The living – they praise YOU, as I am doing today;

parents tell your children about GOD's faithfulness."

Isaiah 38:17-19 (NIV)

Chapter One

INSIGHTFUL TRUTHS

INSIGHT into the 7 PRINCIPLES of SELF

Your I~N~N~E~R BEAUTY is the beliefs you keep in your 'thoughts and heart' about your personal SELF, and the actions you project from those beliefs before others.

The 7 PRINCIPLES of SELF are the seven different guiding logics into your basic conduct and management within your beliefs.

Ladies, have a pen and a highlighter pen handy to mark in this book what speaks to you, so you can return to those areas at any time to refresh your new-found 7 Principles of SELF and more!

The theme throughout this book is about getting to know your I~N~N~E~R SELF; your I~N~N~E~R BEAUTY. You do this by discovering what GOD has already created within you that you may not even know how to use or actually realized they existed.

We must know SELF in-depth in order to be able to make needed changes and then we must know MIND and HEART to know... what to let go of and what to enhance in our lives!

I know most Ladies don't like to talk about SELF, but I think you'll soon see the importance in why we need to know all about the I~N~N~E~R BEAUTY RECIPE – the 7 Principles of SELF, that's within our inner beliefs. Ladies, once you have the total knowledge of your I~N~N~E~R BEAUTY, you will have a strong desire to experience more of it!

Your I~N~N~E~R BEAUTY makes you valuable to GOD, because it's the way HE created you to begin with. Therefore, knowing it will also make you valuable to yourself and to others, when you allow it to shine through you.

Did you know your I~N~N~E~R BEAUTY can heal a torn spirit? It can also build, or rebuild, a broken life into a positive life and much more. The I~N~N~E~R BEAUTY GOD created within us is there to build up our strength and intensify our power to accomplish our goals! It is because of the I~N~N~E~R BEAUTY LOVE ... from GOD!

LADIES, LET HIM WORK HIS GLORIOUS POWERS WITHIN YOU!!!!

Ask yourself these three questions...

- Where do I place my **definition** of beauty?
- Is it the same way I **identify** my beauty?
- What is the **present vision** for my I~N~N~E~R SELF Image?

Did your answers come out to be pleasant and pleasing responses? Throughout this book, our goal is to learn more about our personal identity as a Lady, and as a child of the KING. We'll learn about facing life and living life, with more...

- Confidence and Motivation, because they always help us reach our goals and dreams in life... what we desire to accomplish.
- Fulfillment from our intentions and our accomplishments that helps bring us more into...
- GOD's likeness; overall... what He created us to be from day one in our lives.

You will see the word... SELF many, many times, while reading through these pages. Years back, I was told by a good friend of mine, after the second night of teaching this Bible study, that

I was talking about SELF too much. She told me, "It shouldn't be about SELF, it should be about GOD."

She told me that all my talk about SELF was making her somewhat uncomfortable. I explained that was the whole message... talking about our SELF, so we will know and understand our personal beliefs at a deeper level. Even our deep beliefs that we've had hidden away for many years need to be examined. We need to know where they came from and why we allow some to take over the truths! Because, if we don't know what and why we believe the things we do about ourselves, our I~N~N~E~R Beliefs, then how are we going to know what needs to be changed, adjusted, renewed, adopted, and last, but not least ... LET GO OF? After a couple more classes, my friend finally understood why knowing about SELF is very important!

Yes, there's going to be a lot of talk about SELF, but, Ladies... Only you can make the decision to CHANGE what needs to change in your I~N~N~E~R Beliefs. JESUS does the changing within us, but first we have to be willing for the changes to take place. See Ladies, it begins with us! We are the only ones that can make the decision to allow GOD into our Hearts and allow HIM to change us. No one else has that power. No one else lives in our bodies. And, no one else can live our life. So, how do you want to live yours?

NOTE... You may not understand why I sometimes I spell the word INNER like this: I~N~N~E~R. Look at it this way, the ~ is an indication of 'depth'. Therefore, seeing the word, I~N~N~E~R, means going deeper within your thoughts and heart with having a better awareness of your beliefs. By seeing it displayed like this, you will remember what your I~N~N~E~R deep beliefs are supposed to be... POSITIVE!

WHAT DOES GOD DESIRE FROM US?

Our GOD wants us to develop our I~N~N~E~R Self into more of HIS LIKENESS! And, you know HIS likeness is ALWAYS on the positive side, so what side do we see ourselves... the negative side or the positive side of Life? HE is right here with us to help us reach our goals.

First off, we must realize and understand what all the *junk* is in our brains and hearts, in order to make the changes. When you hear or read something that's said to be a negative statement toward you, STOP IT right then from entering into your Belief-System! Begin right then saying this three times... GO AWAY NEGATIVES...GO AWAY NEGATIVES... GO AWAY NEGATIVES!

And, then raise your arms toward heaven and begin to pray for GOD'S shield of protection from the negative narrative. GOD will help you keep the junk from entering into your

Belief-System, because all these negative words, thoughts and beliefs that are thrown at you are from satan. (I never capitalize the word satan – give satan no honor.)

HOW'S IT WORKING OUT with TRYING TO LEAVE the NEGATIVES BEHIND?

I want to share with you this poem I wrote several years ago but it still holds very strong suggestions for us to follow. Read very closely the words about our negative beliefs. I'm talking about our baggage/our suitcases of junk that we carry around every day! Now this is one thing you need to allow your brain and your heart to hear!

THE BELIEF-RELIEF POEM

You think you can pack them up and leave 'em on your sofa at home as you walk out the door;
Or leave 'em in your car when you go into the store;
Or pack 'em in a box and put 'em away in a closet or attic and leave 'em there.
You just can't do that, Ladies, so beware!
Be extra careful what you feed into your brain and heart because in so many ways...
That of which you store in these two personal, powerful devices about yourself is with you 24 hours for many days.
Because, it doesn't take much to be convinced that nothing

will ever change in your Belief,

And for the rest of your life you carry all the un-truths about yourself, without any Relief!

That's why GOD has given me this message to share with each of you today,

To help you see and believe how wonderfully made you are from the inside–out as HIS Beautiful Creation, and HE will show you the way...

To let go of all that negative thinking, and saying... "Oh well, that's just who I believe I am – It's too late to change me now", but my Sisters, you're WRONG.

Listen, GOD desires you to become a new creation into the image that He has planned for you all ALONG!!!!

Yes, I know it...

I'm not much of a poet!

But there's so much truth within those words of rhyme,

If we would only take them to Heart, we would see it all in time!

THE END!!

Hey, we can have a little light 'serious' humor mixed in with all the other seriousness! Right? But, did you get the message in the poem? (Go back and read it again.)

Ladies, GOD will show us the way to leave all the negative thoughts and beliefs in HIS hands, so that we will be free from them and they will never be picked up and stored back into our Belief-System again. Hallelujah!

Chapter One Reflections

My I~N~N~E~R BEAUTY that GOD created within me builds up my STRENGTH and intensifies my POWER to accomplish my goals! It is because of the I~N~N~E~R BEAUTY LOVE ... from GOD! JESUS does the changing within us, but first I have to be willing for the changes to take place. WHAT DOES GOD DESIRE FROM ME? He wants me to develop my I~N~N~E~R-Self into more of HIS likeness.

At this moment in my Journey-Walk, how beautiful does my I~N~N~E~R BEAUTY make me feel?

Where do I place my definition of beauty?

Is it the same way I identify my beauty?

What is the 'present vision' for my SELF Image?

Who is the only one who can make the decision to CHANGE what is needing to be changed in my negative thoughts and beliefs?

Taking into account my negative beliefs that I've allowed to be attached to me, what are they saying about me and to others?

What are we to say out loud three times when satan throws 'negative words of destruction' at us?

PRAY THIS PRAYER EVERYDAY: "GOD, show me the way to leave all the negative thoughts and beliefs in YOUR hands, so that I will be free from them. Help me to NEVER pick them up again and store them back into my BELIEF-SYSTEM! Place YOUR SHIELD of PROTECTION AROUND ME. AMEN."

Ladies, as you go through your day each day, meditate on these questions and the way you answered them, and never forget to PRAY.

NOTE TAKING SPACE

Chapter Two

WHAT DO WE TAKE WITH US EVERYWHERE WE GO?

Ladies, what do we carry around with us 'every step' we take? When we walk through a door, into any room or store, sitting on a sofa chilling out, driving or riding in a vehicle, or walking in a wide-open field, what do we take with us everywhere we go? No, I'm not talking about our purses, cellphones or other electronics!

I know what you're probably thinking at this moment, "What in the world is she talking about"?

Let's explore the answer, and it's really very simple. What do we take with us everywhere we go, every moment of the day, in our Belief-System?

OUR BELIEF SYSTEM IS OUR... BRAIN & HEART

The paragraph below will be the most mindful words you'll read throughout this book! So, Ladies, copy and paste these words in your memory storage!

Your **Belief-System** consists of your Brain and your Heart. When words pass through your brain, you either let them pass on through 'one-ear-and-out-the other' OR you place them into your beliefs and allow them to go to your Heart, which 'stores your beliefs'! Same with the thoughts that enters your brain.

*READ the paragraph again so you totally understand the transaction.

Have you realized everything that is in your BRAIN supports your Beliefs Thoughts, and everything you have stored in your HEART that you believe about yourself, goes with you every inch of your movement and every second of the day? Every time you walk into any room, or exit any door, when you're sitting still, walking out in a wide-open field or riding in a vehicle, everywhere you go, ALL those BELIEFS in your MIND and HEART are right there with you – 86,400 seconds a day – 1,440 minutes a day – 24 hours a day – 7 days a week – 12 months a year! Ladies, is that not an eye-opener?

Now, let's read this out loud, so you can really absorb it ...

Everywhere I go, every step I step, I take everything I think I know about myself, that has been stored in my brain/mind over my lifetime. Everywhere I go, I take everything I believe in my heart about myself... both POSITIVE or NEGATIVE!

You can't leave your Belief-System behind, it's impossible! That's as simple as it gets! But, is it that simple?

In our Belief-System, the **BRAIN** is our **thought processing computer**, and the **HEART** is our **belief hard drive!** Both have the capacity to 'hold' all our **BELIEFS**. So, for this reason, they are our '**STORAGE UNITS**'.

These STORAGE UNITS, that you are born with, hold what you think of yourself as a person and a Lady. They play a very important part in your life, every second of every day. The beliefs you store in your mind and in your heart about who you are can be separated into three categories:

1. **BENEFICIAL BELIEFS**- (Positive Beliefs) These are Beliefs which allows you to think Positive thoughts about yourself.

2. **NOT SO BENEFICIAL BELIEFS**- (Not so

Beneficial) These are Beliefs which keeps you questioning your abilities, strengths and importance.

3. **DESTRUCTIVE BELIEFS**- (Negative Beliefs) These are Beliefs which can best be described as 'pull me down – keep me down' negative-Beliefs. Makes you live within Journey-Crawls!

Which Beliefs do you find crossing your mind daily? Beneficial? Not so beneficial? Or, downright destructive? No matter which belief category you find yourself in, Beliefs are stored into your Belief-System and, at some point, will announce to others that this is who you believe you are!

Ladies, we're never without our Belief-System, so shouldn't we be placing our focus on the POSITIVES, and remove all the negatives? Life would be much easier going if we could. And, remember this... LIFE is too short to be carrying around all those negative Beliefs!

UNDERSTAND THIS PROCESS... Once we've heard or read statements, positive or negative, that someone has said to us or about us, our BRAIN takes it in. Then, eventually, that statement will settle into our HEARTS as a deep-embedded belief, unless we have our shield up to protect us from the

NEGATIVES. Unless we block out all the NEGATIVE verbiage.

When our beliefs go down into our Hearts, it's hard to delete them. Why? It may be that we don't want to delete them, for one reason or another! We've grown comfortable with these thoughts, even if they are negative. Another reason could be that we don't know how to rid ourselves of them. We're so used to thinking a certain way that thinking differently would require reprogramming. Unless we have a change of Heart (a reprogramming), these Beliefs, Positive and Negative, will go to the grave with us! What will you be carrying within you, up until you take your last breath? Something to think about, isn't it?

Let's go a step deeper. Knowing you now have a Belief-System within your body, consisting of your brain and heart. What are you storing in these two systems?

The message here is... an ASSET is to be viewed and taken in as a significant valuable benefit! INACCURACIES (incorrectness) are all the negative thoughts that are a waste of space in our beliefs. And, when we give them power in our lives, they wreak havoc in our Belief-System, destroying everything that our CREATOR has intended to be blessings in our lives, because we tend to believe the incorrectness.

- ASSETS... a useful entity of quality expected to provide future benefits.
- ENTITY... something that has a real existence (data that's considered significant).
- INACCURACIES... a state of 'not being accurate.'

Seriously, Ladies, there are ASSETS and INACCURACIES that we carry with us 24/7, that are stored in our Belief-System! These beliefs are shaping how we think about ourselves and who we believe we have the potential to become. Wouldn't you want to kick out the INACCURACIES (the waste) and protect the ASSETS at all cost?

Shouldn't they be useful qualities in our lives, because we're never without them! These ASSETS make up the person we think, or we truly believe, we are, as a Lady as a human being. And, they should be providing us future benefits. Do I have your attention yet?

WHY MAYBE YOUR MIND and HEART CHANGE MAY NOT HAVE HAPPENED YET

Maybe you're thinking, "CJ, I already know negative thoughts and beliefs that I have are bad, but I just haven't been able to kick them." I hear you. I have been there myself. Listed below might be some of the reasons why updating your Belief-System hasn't happened yet in your life.

1. UNCLEAR BELIEFS: The need to change may not be clear to you, as of yet. You've lived with these beliefs this long, so they're obviously a part of who you are at this point, right? How would you be able to separate what is negative and positive? What is true and untrue? "I can understand that, hopefully, this book will be of great help."

2. COMFORTABLE BELIEFS: Maybe you know the thoughts and beliefs that need to be changed in your own life, but the WILLINGNESS to change them is not yet there on your part. This has the same feel as the unclear Beliefs, only these are a bit more dangerous. Rather than accepting them, just because you've always had them and aren't sure what you truly believe, you've taken it to another level. You are not sure what you would do without them. "Believe me, I've been there!"

3. LET'S CHANGE BELIEFS: Or maybe, just maybe, you are well aware of these negative thoughts that have taken up residence in your STORAGE UNITS. As you are reading these words, you can immediately list some of them. You haven't had any idea how to kick them to the curb before, but YOU'RE NOW READY!

Let's sing HALLELUJAH! Because that is exactly the place you need to be to get everything this book has to offer. A place where you are ready to learn how to let negative thoughts go and change the pathway in your lives. Creating a more Confident and Positive walk, with CHRIST as your Guide.

With that said, Ladies, I have high expectations that wherever you find that you're strong, or weak, within the 7 PRINCIPLES of 'SELF', you will allow GOD to do great wonders in your life! You will soon have The CONFIDENCE WALK & POSTURE IN CHRIST you so desire to experience, because the I~N~N~E~R BEAUTY within you will now shine through! I pray this for you!

Hopefully there will be several reasons why you'll look forward to reading each chapter. Whatever the reason, GOD may be bringing HIS plan into focus for your MIND-SET to focus differently, your HEART-LOVE to be stronger for yourself, and for your entire LIFE to change in a blissful way.

Just so you know, I refuse to compromise GOD's Word and message, for the sake of the way the world sees what a Lady should be or how she should present herself in today's society. Today's Ladies need to hear the truth, and I warn you now about the incredible truths that GOD has put on my Heart to write into this book. There will be more honesty on my part than I have been comfortable to write about. But, yet, I still wrote about my weaknesses, my struggles, and my baggage throughout my lifetime, including those in the present that I still struggle with daily that I'm sure some of you can relate to as well.

Right now, I don't want you to get a brain overload! We're going to take it one step at a time, as we go further into our I~N~N~E~R BEAUTY with 'The 7 Principles of 'SELF'.

Whatever the reason you have picked up this book, I say... WELCOME! I'm excited to walk with you throughout this journey!

Read this statement out loud...

Everywhere I go, I take everything I KNOW and BELIEVE ABOUT MYSELF! Everything that is in my Brain that supports my Belief Thoughts; and everything that is in my Heart that I think I truly Believe about myself... goes with me everywhere I go. All my Beliefs, from Head-to-Heart, of how I see myself, they ALL walk with me every step I take!
- A CJism

Keep the above words in your Minds and Hearts at all times! What's in your Personal Belief-System that walks with you every hour of every day of every month of every year? Something to think and ponder about, isn't it? We'll be doing a lot of thinking and pondering about that statement throughout this book!

Let's REVIEW...

- BELIEF-SYSTEM/STORAGE UNITS- Our MINDS & HEARTS.
- ASSETS- a 'useful entity of quality' expected to provide future benefits – Positive thoughts we have stored in our BELIEF-SYSTEM.
- ENTITY- something that has a real existence (data that's considered significant).
- INACCURACIES- a state of 'not being accurate' ERRORS = the negative thoughts we have stored in our BELIEF-SYSTEM.

Ladies, what BELIEFS are you carrying around with you? What BELIEFS are strongly attached to you?

LET'S CARRY THIS THOUGHT WITH US...

Once we pinpoint, and then release, all the INACCURACIES (negative Beliefs), it's endless what we can accomplished with our 'TRUE SELF' that GOD has known all along! Ladies, once the Negatives are GONE, LEAVE THEM THERE...

NEVER TO BE PICKED UP AGAIN!!!

GOD sent the spirit of HIS SON into our Hearts, the Spirit who calls out, "ABBA, FATHER." So, you are no longer a slave, but GOD's child; and since you are HIS child, GOD has made you also an heir.   Galatians 4:6-7

Chapter Two Reflections

What I believe as the TRUTH about myself is stored in my Brain and Heart which is called my Belief-System. Everywhere I go I take everything I know and Believe ABOUT MYSELF! Everything that is in my Brain that supports my Belief Thoughts; and everything that is in my Heart that I think I truly Believe about myself... goes with me everywhere I go. All my Beliefs, from Head to Heart, of how I see myself, they are with me every step I take!

Are these BELIEFS with me at all times, 24/7?

What is the most I have stored away in my Belief-System? The POSITIVE or the NEGATIVE? And why?

What are three NEGATIVE BELIEFS about myself that I'd truly like to rid myself from now, and WHY do I have these beliefs?

Are all MY PERSONAL THOUGHTS and BELIEFS I have about myself USEFUL or HARMFUL to my existence?

Are they 'PROVIDING' ME FUTURE BENEFITS or PRESENT OBSTRUCTION?

Are they 'PRODUCING' TO INCREASE 'VALUE' into MY JOURNEY-WALK or WEAKNESSES to keep me 'TORN DOWN'?

Do I 'TAKE ALL my THOUGHTS and BELIEFS for GRANTED' without any assessment to the amount of WORTH or DESTRUCTION it can add TO MY EXISTENCE? Why or why not?

SOMETHING TO THINK ABOUT... How do we determine the answers to the questions above? It's Simple.... Our BELIEFS about our SELF that are in our BRAINS & HEARTS, are they NEGATIVE or POSITIVE Assets?

How are you with walking away from the Negatives in your life and leaving them?

PRAY, PRAY AND PRAY SOME MORE!

NOTE TAKING SPACE

Chapter Three

DO NOT LIE TO YOUR SELF!

Our theme verse for this Chapter and our lasting goal will be, **"Do not lie to each other, since you have taken off your old self with its practices and have put on the new self, which is being renewed in knowledge in the image of its Creator" Colossians 3:9-10 (NIV)**

Paul wrote this in his letter to the Colossians on the rules for Holy Living. Although he states, "Do not lie to each other..." he also says... "since you have taken off your old self..." So, with that I'd like to expand the statement to further say, "Do not lie to yourself". I think GOD would be okay with that addition. Don't you? You're about to see why these five words play a large importance in our day-to-day Journey-Walk as we go forward in this book.

My prayer for each of you right now is... by the time you finish this book, GOD will have revealed to you what it means to take off your old self with its practices and put on the new self, which is being renewed in knowledge in the image of its Creator. We all, me included, have plenty of old-self practices to rid ourselves from!

Do not lie to yourself thinking you're not worthy of having, and enjoying, all that GOD has for you from within your I~N~N~E~R BEAUTY is a restless and unnecessary place to be! Our LORD has already begun a good work in you, at your birth. And, Ladies, HE is not finished with you yet! So, don't give up!

Our goal is to learn more about our own identity as a beautiful Lady, and most of all as a... Child of the King of all Kings. Together, let's learn that facing life with more confidence and hopefulness, and having a strong spiritual will, Mind and Heart will help us reach our goals within our dreams. It will also bring us more into GOD's likeness. Are we, or are we not, Ladies searching to be more like the Lady GOD created us to be in the first place? I hope your answer was a brazenly, YES!

You read it a few pages back, but let's look at this again... WHAT DOES GOD DESIRE FROM US? HE wants you and I to develop our I~N~N~E~R Self into more of HIS LIKENESS! And, you know HIS likeness is ALWAYS on the POSITIVE SIDE. So, where do you see yourself... on the Negative side or Positive side of Life?

Ladies, let's stop lying to ourselves. For if we only knew all the blessings we're missing out on when we live a life of denial, and in an unnecessary-negative self-imaging-bubble, we would be totally overwhelmed! Once you have seen bits and pieces of your I~N~N~E~R BEAUTY, you will have a strong desire to understand and see more of it! Our I~N~N~E~R BEAUTY, that makes us valuable in GOD's eyes, will also make us valuable to ourselves.

And, last but not least, it will make us valuable to others! Don't lie to yourself; because your I~N~N~E~R BEAUTY is more beautiful than the face of any beauty queen; the most beautiful super model that ever walked the runway or graced the pages of magazines; and any Hollywood or theater stage actress! Let me hear an "AMEN!"

Does that not light a fire inside your Minds and Hearts to desire and understand more about your I~N~N~E~R BEAUTY?

"Being confident of this, that HE who has begun a good work in you will carry it on to completion until the day you see CHRIST JESUS." Philippians 1:6 (NIV)

LET'S CARRY THIS THOUGHT WITH US...

To paraphrase a statement I once heard... When GOD made woman, He didn't create her from the outside in... He created her from the inside out.

Ladies, you and I need to know what it is that GOD has placed within us, before birth because remember... HE makes NO mistakes, and HE makes NO junk! Allow GOD to do a good work in you.

Chapter Three Reflections

Thinking I'm not worthy of having and enjoying all that GOD has for me from within my I~N~N~E~R BEAUTY is a RESTLESS and UN-necessary place to be! GOD has already begun a good work in me, at my birth, and 'HE' is not FINISHED with me yet! I'm looking forward to learning more on facing LIFE with more confidence and hopefulness, and having a strong spiritual will, Mind and Heart that will help ME reach more goals within MY dreams. It will also bring me more into GOD's LIKENESS. Talking about my 'SELF' will help me know and understand my Self-Beliefs at a deeper LEVEL.

Do the images I have of myself right at this moment resemble GOD in any way? If your answer is No, what do you think will be your course of action to change those images?

Don't lie to myself; because my I~N~N~E~R BEAUTY is more beautiful than...

How are we going to know which SELF-Beliefs need to be thrown out, if we don't ask GOD to reveal them to us? This may be a problem as well.

What does GOD desire from us?

NOTE TAKING SPACE

The following page is a list of our CHAPTERS of INGREDIENTS. We will be going into each INGREDIENT with deep discussion. I will be explaining how our I~N~N~E~R BEAUTY works within us to a deeper level. Are you ready? Let's jump right in... Becoming A Confident Lady of Purpose.

THE 7 PRINCIPLES of 'SELF'...

"THE INNER BEAUTY RECIPE"

| **SELF-CONCEPT** | 1ST PRINCIPLE | HOW WE SEE OURSELVES OVER ALL... |

| **SELF-RESPECT** **SELF-LOVE** | 2nd & 3rd PRINCIPLES | INGREDIENTS #1 & #2 |

| **SELF-ESTEEM** **SELF-MOTIVATION** | 4th & 5th PRINCIPLES | INGREDIENTS #3 & #4 |

| **SELF-CONFIDENCE** | 6th PRINCIPLE | INGREDIENT #5 |

With & Through GOD, all the above equals...

| OUR... **SELF-WORTH !!!** | 7th PRINCIPLE | INGREDIENT #6 - OUR RESULTS |

Chapter Four

I~N~N~E~R BEAUTY RECIPE

The Ingredients 'In Life' – Our SOURCES

Definition to... Recipe... a set of 'instructions' for making or preparing something; 'a go to source'. (Wikapedia, 2020)

"LIFE IS LIKE A BOX OF RECIPES..."

GOD has already provided us with the RECIPE (instructions) and all the ingredients to live LIFE. Ladies, it's up to us to follow them. We need to follow the RECIPE, and then share with others what our I~N~N~E~R ingredients, that GOD has placed within each of us, is all about.

Here's an eye opener... Our Brains & Hearts, along with our... Eyes, Ears and Voices (Mouths), are of vital importance to us in so many ways. We may need to learn how to bring them forth and 'learn' how to live with them in a more Positive and blissful way! Why? Because, they are so very important to our existence! It's the matter of how strong each ingredient is within us that's going to determine how strong, or how weak, our inward beliefs of I~N~N~E~R BEAUTY really are!

OUR GO-TO-SOURCES

Let's say you woke up one morning and decided to bake a cake to enjoy later that day. What's the first thing you do? Decide on which flavor and size of cake you want to bake. Right? You then search the kitchen for the ingredients and discover several items that you'll need. You grab your purse and keys and run to the grocery store and pick up what you need, so you'll have all the ingredients.

The grocery store can be considered as your GO-TO SOURCE to supply all that is needed to accomplish this quest of making the cake you so desire to have.

In reference to LIFE... We all have available to us our...GO-TO-SOURCES. So, Ladies, we're going to be... "Going-To-Our-Sources" to find many answers! I'm sure you're asking... what are our GO–TO– SOURCES? Let's look at them...

- GOD... the Author of the WORD... the SOURCE
- The BIBLE... the written WORD of GOD... our RESOURCE
- PRAYER... is our COURSE... to help us stay on COURSE with our SOURCE

- CHRISTIAN FRIENDS who are grounded in GOD's WORD
- GOD's CHRISTIAN LEADERS... Pastors, Teachers, Authors and all who are spreading the WORD of GOD 'from the BIBLE'!

We're going to go through the outline of the ingredients first, then go into deep examination with each one separately, as you see on the INDEX SHEET.

FROM the BOWL to the ICING:
WHAT IS A RECIPE?

The Bowl that Holds It All... Self-CONCEPT

Standard Mixing...the BOWLS and UTENSILS of Life!

In order to make a cake, we must have a mixing bowl to place all the ingredients in. Also, we must have the correct measuring utensils. We mix the cake in the bowl and then pour the batter into the baking pan. Right?

We're mixing together all the ingredients in the bowl, to which we are referring as our Self-Concept. Why a bowl? Because the 'bowl' is the symbol of 'holding' all the ingredients. Whereas, in this scenario, it holds all that is within our Belief-System, our Minds and Hearts, the Positives and the Negatives thoughts and beliefs. Sometimes we mistake something in the recipe and throw bad ingredients into our bowl (negative thoughts). Have you ever measured out the salt and added to the bowl when it should have been sugar? That will throw a recipe totally off!

Same as what we may do within our Self-CONCEPT. We throw something negative into our thoughts and it soon becomes a belief about ourselves that is an unnecessary and false belief and throws our POSITIVE BELIEFS off; out of kilter. Then it is 'mixed into our beliefs' that we carry around as the truth.

Now, let's look at the 6 different action topics of ingredients as an outline of our I~N~N~E~R BEAUTY...

First Ingredient... FLOUR

The Cake RECIPE... Flour... One of the main ingredients used to make a cake is... FLOUR. This additive in a recipe is used as a thickening agent. I like to call it 'FLOUR-POWER'! FLOUR is obviously the essential ingredient. If we don't have enough FLOUR, our cake won't have much substance. But, if we have too much flour, our cake will be hard to swallow. We need to ensure that we have just the right amount of flour for the recipe.

The Personal RECIPE #1. **Self-RESPECT** ... How much do we RESPECT our own being? Starting with... RESPECTING our minds, our Hearts, our values, our relationships with GOD and with people, and the least enjoyable for us to talk about is...how much do we RESPECT our bodies?

Ask yourself these questions...

- What do I allow into my mind and heart that's DISRESPECTFUL to my own being?
- Do I RESPECT myself enough not to allow others to hurt or destroy my positive I~N~N~E~R thoughts and beliefs about myself?
- Can I filter out the negatives that may be trying to enter into my heart? Because, once in my brain, it won't take long for 'words of destruction' to enter into the core of my heart. And, then it's hard to rid myself of the negatives.
- How much RESPECT do I give myself over all?

Now that the FLOUR is in our Mixing Bowl... let's look at the next ingredient...

Second Ingredient... SUGAR

The Cake RECIPE... Sugar... We all like sugar, right? And, we all know what SUGAR brings to a RECIPE...SWEETNESS! But, it also gives the item you're cooking its texture. It keeps baked goods soft and moist, creating tenderness. Just think of this... if you're mixing up something you are going to be baking, like a cake or cookies without sugar or a sugar substitute, there is a possibility that it will give you shivers upon taking a bite of it... and not in a good way! YUCK! Without sugar, not only would our cake or cookies not be sweet, but it wouldn't bake at all to be recognizable.

The Personal RECIPE # 2. Self-LOVE ... When we LOVE ourselves, we present ourselves with dignity and poise, so that others take notice there is something different and great inside of us. We must ask ourselves... "How much do I LOVE myself?" Whaaaat? Now, that's not a question you ask yourself every day! Is it? But, go ahead, ask yourself right now... "How much do I LOVE MYSELF?" You may be thinking... "How do, and how can, I LOVE my-own-self? How can I make my

LIFE sweet and recognizable with Self-Love? Good question! We'll learn more about what GOD intended for us to believe about HIS love and HIS desires for us to LOVE ourselves as we continue in this book. But, for now, let's move along to the next ingredient...

Third Ingredient... BUTTER

The Cake RECIPE... Butter ... Butter is the key ingredient for flavor. It also makes the batter tender and helps in leavening (making it rise).

The Personal RECIPE #3. Self-ESTEEM ... Is your Self-ESTEEM on a 'high' level of rising up to produce what you're needing to stay POSITIVE during your Journey-Walk through life? Self-Esteem is the ingredient we need in our lives to help "make us rise." Do you hear it frequently of someone having "high" Self-Esteem? All too often, people are typically referred to as having low self-Esteem.

Some people refer to Esteem as 'energy'. "My Self-Esteem is in high gear today!" It also can be referred to as... satisfaction in oneself, or favorable opinion and of value. "We all know that self-esteem (sometimes referred to as self-worth or self-respect) can be an important part of success. Too little self-esteem can leave people feeling defeated or depressed. It can also lead people to make bad choices, fall into destructive relationships, or fail to live up to their full potential". – Kendra Cherry (Cherry, 2019)

Can you relate to any of that statement? What you allow to enter into your Brains & Hearts will have a NEGATIVE or POSTIVE effect on your Self-Esteem, which is why we must be so careful of what we allow into our 'Bowl of Life.'

Fourth Ingredient... VANILLA

The Cake RECIPE... Vanilla... This ingredient tastes terrible by itself. But, adding it to other ingredients enhances all the other flavors in the recipe. Without it, baked goods will taste flat and bland. It's the Baker's best friend! Vanilla isn't just there to add flavor, but to enhance all the flavors around it.

The Personal RECIPE #4. Self-MOTIVATION... Our Self-Motivation enhances everything else we're doing.

This is why the first three ingredients are so important to our LIFE recipe. If we lack Self-Respect, Self-Love, and Self-Esteem, there is nothing that Self-Motivation can enhance. Our Motivation will only become a STRONG WILL if the above three ingredients are strong in our life. Think of it this way... We think we have a desire to get something accomplished that could add a wonderful and Positive change in our lives, but then...

- All these negative beliefs we've stored in our minds and Hearts begin to arise, reminding us of past failures, And, we quickly fall into non-energy discouragement.

- Then there's the words we're taking into our Belief-System from people that have offered us nothing but negative things, which has halted our motivation. Or, we look in the mirror and cannot say one nice thing about ourselves.

- We remember we have no respect or love for ourselves so, therefore, our Self-Esteem is low, offering us no Motivation toward proceeding to try and accomplish our desires and dreams!

Do you see the belief pattern here? How sad is this? Ladies, how often has this happened in your life?

Fifth Ingredient... EGGS

The Cake RECIPE... Eggs... play an important role in whatever the recipe is; they create structure and stability within a batter. They help thicken and emulsify, and also add moisture – they act like the glue that holds the cake together.

The Personal RECIPE #5. Self-CONFIDENCE ... This is the ingredient that holds our efforts together, until our mission is finished.

There are different ways people use "CONFIDENCE" to describe situations or conditions. Here are some examples...

- "She has a lot of Self-Confidence in herself. So, she will accomplish her goals because her self-Esteem is high." She has Self-Confidence!
- "I wish I had more Self-Confidence, so I can accomplish something great in my life. But, I don't have any Self-

Motivation!" when, in this last case, this person has low to no self-Esteem nor Self-Motivation!

- "I am confident I can make this deal work for you." Having and sharing the confidence.
- "At the moment, she's going through a rough patch. She's a very confident Lady and I can see her holding it all together." A Lady with a Purpose!

Having strong Self-Confidence in one's self can only happen when the first four ingredients are in place and strong.

Ladies, when we lack CONFIDENCE, we'll find ourselves lacking structure and stability. Again, there is an order to how we add these ingredients to our personal life. If we lack the first four ingredients, there's nothing to bring forth Self-Confidence! Yes, we may be weak in one Principle, but with strong-willed in other Principles will build the weaker up to a higher level.

Sixth Ingredient... The ICING

Self-Worth... The ICING... The sixth ingredient is our "umph". Our icing on the cake – our icing in LIFE!

The Personal RECIPE #6. Self-Worth... Our Self-Concept, Respect, Love, Esteem, Motivation and Confidence need to be strong in order to build a strong foundation for our Self-Worth. All 6 INGREDIENTS are to be used to accomplish our goals in life! Our Self-Worth is the "GET UP AND MAKE IT HAPPEN" in life. Our icing on the cake!

You cannot truly feel you have a lasting Self-Worth without ALL six ingredients; one building upon the other that gives you the true feeling of Self-Worth! You can't put icing on your cake until there is a CAKE! Can you?

Why do I call it THE I~N~N~E~R BEAUTY RECIPE? Because, to understand your entire beliefs within yourself, you must understand how each ingredient of the RECIPE works – starting with...

- Self-Concept... An overall belief of what YOU see and believe about YOUR-SELF. **"I can do all things through CHRIST who gives me strength." Philippians 4:13 (NIV)**
- Self-Respect... Respecting what GOD has created within YOU to become. **"In the same way, the women are to be worthy of RESPECT, not malicious talkers but temperate and trustworthy in everything." 1 Timothy 3:11 (NIV)**
- Self-Love... Loving the person YOU can become in

LIFE and in CHRIST. **"And now abide faith, hope, love, these three, but the greatest is LOVE." 1 Corinthians 13:13 (KJV)**

- Self-Esteem... Believing YOU can do IT. Whatever 'IT' is. **"FAITH can move mountains." Matthew 17:20 (NIV)**

- Self-Motivation... Getting up – making it happen – because of your own enthusiasm, interest, and believing YOU CAN DO IT because CHRIST is with you! **"I can do ALL things through CHRIST who strengthens me." Philippians 4:13 (NIV)**

- Self-Confidence... A feeling of TRUST in my abilities and judgements – having SELF-ASSURANCE. **"CONFIDENCE shall be your strength." Isaiah 30:15b (KJV)**

- Self-Worth... I AM A 'SOMEBODY' in CHRIST- **"Don't be afraid; you are WORTH more than many sparrows." Luke 12:7 (NIV)**

Do you have a better understanding now of what ingredients the I~N~N~E~R BEAUTY RECIPE is made with and why? Do you have a better understanding how we must know and understand all the ingredients and our abilities within us? If we don't follow a recipe, step-by-step, every ingredient cannot do its best to produce a great and Positive outcome.

Just like in our lives... if we don't follow what is written in the Bible, in applying the best of ourselves that's already within us, the outcome will tell itself. Explanation... Whether we're following the RECIPE in creating something extraordinary, we will have 'items' that must be 'mixed' together. Right? 'The I~N~N~E~R BEAUTY RECIPE' is made up of several different 'items' in the mix!

Ladies, plan on meeting GOD throughout the pages of this book! He has something for each one of us to read and believe in. We need to take it to Heart and apply what we've learned to our everyday LIFE-JOURNEY-WALK. Then, sharing it with others will take us deeper into our FATHER'S image.

LET'S CARRY THIS THOUGHT WITH US...

LIFE is a RECIPE. We need all the ingredients and the right amount in order to become the person that we, and most importantly... GOD, so desires us to be! GOD has provided us with all the ingredients and the instructions, now it is up to 'us' to follow them in order to become the beautiful creation HE has had planned for us all along... that GOD created us for from the beginning!

Chapter Four Reflections

"I'm a SOMEBODY" – or – "I'm a NOBODY!" Which statement do you say about yourself?

The world lays out before us in... TV shows and news, movies, and the social media what we are to believe about ourselves? But should we live by the world's opinions or by GOD's plans for our lives? Why?

In the list of Self-INGREDIENTS, which one(s) are you the strongest in applying? Explain to yourself WHY.

In the list of Self-INGREDIENTS, which one(s) do you struggle with the most? Explain to yourself WHY.

In your own words... Explain what a RECIPE is.

Is the I~N~N~E~R Beauty RECIPE a strong "LIGHT" in your walk with GOD? Explain your answer.

NOTE TAKING SPACE

PART 'A'

BELIEVING WORDS of STATEMENTS

ACCEPTANCE	CONVINCED	CERTAINTY IN CONFIDENCE

PART 'B'

WHAT ARE MY *"BELIEF WORDS"*?

MY 'BELIEF WORDS' *same as...* MY 'IT'S' / MY 'TAG-ALONGS'	TAKING UP SPACE IN MY STORAGE UNITS

PART 'C'

OUR BELIEF PROCESS

BELIEF-PROCESS-SYSTEM	INNER-SELF-BELIEFS	LIFE-BELIEF-WALK
1 - EARS & EYES = RECEIVING IN PROCESS 2 - BRAIN & HEART = STORAGE UNITS 3 - MOUTH = OUR TELL-TELL-ALL 4- *Symbol to Detection* = Stinking ___	SELF IMPORTANCE/ **POSITIVES - NEGATIVES**	DOING 'LIFE' – **DO 'I' DO IT WELL?**

Chapter Five

BELIEF WORDS of STATEMENTS

PART 'A'

BELIEVING WORDS of STATEMENTS

ACCEPTANCE	CONVINCED	CERTAINTY IN CONFIDENCE

Statements made by others that you have taken into your beliefs as the truth. From the time we have received these 'Belief Words of Statements' what happens then? Let's discover...

1. **ACCEPTANCE**: Accepting "IT" as the truth.... Whatever "IT" is, Positive or Negative! ("IT", meaning.... "BELIEF WORDS of STATEMENTs").

Words have been spoken to you or about you, and, you are... trying to make up your mind whether to ACCEPT them as the TRUTH or not. The longer you think about it, the more changes it will soon go into your HEART BELIEFS.

Take a few seconds and think back... can you recall a time in the past, or near present, that someone has said something to you – about you, and you believed it. And, sooner or later, you took those words into your Heart as being the truth about yourself. Anyone? Please tell me I'm not the only one who has done this (in my past)!

And then, from that point on, you walked through life 'BELIEVING in that STATEMENT,' whether it was a STATEMENT of Positive or Negative words. You now believe that this STATEMENT is a true description of who you really are! Maybe it affected, one way or another, your Self-Respect, your Self-Esteem, your Self-Motivation, or your Self-Confidence!

For example, you overheard harsh words coming from the mouth of someone you know... "She thinks she can get that job she's applying for, but I don't believe she can! I can't see her in front of people speaking, because she's not smart enough! She doesn't know what she is doing!" Where would this leave you?

Feeling their negative words and believing them? Even if you've had experience with public speaking and qualified for the job, if your lack of confidence is at a low level, it's understandable that you're worried you won't even be considered for the job.

Summing It Up... The message here is, taking ownership in a statement that someone has said about you or to you could do what? Tear your confidence down to the point when you walk into the interview they can tell by your expression and body language you don't have what it takes to succeed in that job. Or, what if, you have the confidence it takes to get the job. And, because of your positiveness, you walk into that room with so much confidence and Self-Motivation that it radiates throughout you the entire meeting!

Ladies, it's all in how you choose to 'ACCEPT the WORDS of STATEMENTS' from others, and what you do with them! Keep and Store them OR let them 'Go in One Ear and Out the Other,' and not allow them to enter into your Belief-System!

2. **CONVINCED**: As in believing 'IT'. Now, I am continuing to accept "IT" because I'm Convinced "IT" is the TRUTH about myself. "IT" meaning...BELIEF WORDS of STATEMENTS. Here again, we've heard WORDS from STATEMENTS about ourselves, maybe the words were said to us as a child or teenager... "You'll never amount to anything!" "No, I will not

allow you to go to college, because you're not smart enough to make it through the first year!" Or, after we're older, we may have heard words like, "You think you're so pretty when in fact you're as ugly as a frog!" You may have been told, "I don't love you and never will! You're a no good, useless person!"

Many people have had parents growing up who never spoke anything Positive into their lives but planted plenty of negative stones that became stumbling blocks later in their lives. Or, we thought we had husbands that loved us, when in fact it was all a show, up until they got what they wanted from us. Or, maybe, a friend that you trusted said harsh untruths about you that were hard to overcome and made it difficult to maintain a Positive attitude and trust anyone else.

Different words, said by others, can be 'swords' to our Hearts that we cannot seem to let go of at all, BECAUSE WE ARE NOW CONVINCED that this is who we are supposed to be. Notice the word 'sword' has 'word' in the spelling. So, therefore, our 'words' can be 'swords' in someone's life! Ladies watch how you use your WORDS when talking to or about someone!

Summing It Up... You have allowed someone's WORDS of STATEMENTS to now be in your BELIEF THOUGHTS, because you are CONVINCED it is the TRUTH about yourself!

3. CERTAINTY IN MY CONFIDENCE: Whether the "ITS" are Positive or Negative... I have Certainty in my Confidence that I Believe "IT" to be the truth about myself!

I AM CONFIDENT! I AM CERTAIN that as I walk through LIFE, as I walk through every door and enter into every room, that what I have taken into my "BELIEF-SYSTEM, IS WHO I AM!" Why? Because it was spoken to me by, maybe, a family member, friend, co-worker, spouse/boyfriend, neighbor, or possibly even a stranger. It could be anyone! I have taken someone's statement and allowed myself to believe "IT," and now I have CERTAINITY in my CONFIDENCE that it is the TRUTH; that this really is WHO I AM!

Are you beginning to see a pattern here within these three definitions? Hint... **Someone else.** We have ALLOWED SOMEONE ELSE to give us a MINDSET in our BELIEFS! You have taken someone's statement and allowed yourself to ACCEPT IT, because you are CONVINCED. And, now you have CERTAINITY In Your CONFIDENCE that it is the TRUTH!

What do all three definitions have in common? ... BELIEF & BELIEVING in someone else's words! Ladies, this is where you will spend LIFE... in Believing Words of Statements!

Will they be Positive or Negative? How do we obtain all these positive and negative beliefs we carry around with us 24 hours a day? Mostly from other people's words, that have been spoken into our lives. Then what happens? We take them in as... BELIEVING WORDS of STATEMENTS!

Within these 5 simple words – ACCEPTANCE, CONVINCED, CERTAINTY in CONFIDENCE, you, myself & I – (notice that I included myself twice) we may have taken ownership in WORDS as being the TRUTH, good and bad, in what others have said to us or about us! They are now known as our BELIEF WORDS!

Do you now see how important these three Actions are to our existence? ACCEPTANCE, CONVINCED, CERTAINTY in CONFIDENCE? The importance of these Actions to our everyday walk in LIFE? Be it NEGATIVE or POSITIVE THINKING & BELIEVING, these BELIEF WORDS begin to overtake our lives, without us even realizing it! Wouldn't you rather have the positives take over, rather than anything else?

YOUR MEMORY VERSE: **Hebrews 13:21 (Revised to personal) I will equip myself with everything good for doing HIS will, and I will allow HIM to work in me what is pleasing to HIM, through JESUS CHRIST, and I will give HIM the glory for ever and ever. Amen**

LET'S CARRY THIS THOUGHT WITH US...

POSITIVITY PRESENT: Ladies, you can be CONQUERORS through our LORD JESUS CHRIST! All things are POSSIBLE THROUGH HIM WHO LOVES US! Let's shout out an... AMEN!

WHAT IS THE POINT HERE? You can do more than you think you can! Believe me, I know that from my own experiences through life. So many people who knows my past cannot believe I would ever be a published author. So, Ladies, you can conquer what you desire to become. You can overcome your PAST and now live in a POSITIVE PRESENT and look forward to an even brighter FUTURE! YOU can conquer your FEARS!

How, you ask?

By BELIEVING GOD CAN AND WILL HELP YOU GET THERE! TRUST HIM! PRAY TO HIM! BELIEVE IN HIM and YOURSELF! And, ALLOW HIM to guide you to the finish line!
And, AND DO YOUR PART! Nothing will ever happen if you sit down and have the attitude... I'll just wait and see if it'll really happen.

"Before I was born, God chose me and called me by HIS marvelous grace."
Galatians 1:15 (NLT)

Chapter Five Reflections

Believing Words of Statements means- Someone has spoken personal words into your life about you –true or false statements – and you've Accepted them, because you are convinced, they are true. You now have Certainty in your Confidence they are words of truth about yourself.

In reference to a spoken FALSE STATEMENT said about you... "Why do you allow SOMEONE to take control over your THOUGHTS and BELIEFS?" How do you allow that to happen?

NOTE TAKING SPACE

Chapter Six

BELIEF WORDS OF STATEMENTS - PARTS B & C

PART 'B'

WHAT ARE MY "BELIEF WORDS"?

MY 'BELIEF WORDS' *same as...* MY 'IT'S' / MY 'TAG-ALONGS'	TAKING UP SPACE IN MY STORAGE UNITS

WHAT ARE MY 'BELIEF WORDS'?

After taking in these 'Words of Statements' that are intended for us – Positive or negative – we most likely turn them into... OUR BELIEF WORDS. We are now convinced that they're the truths about us, and they are now stored in our.... Storage Units! (Now, that is a statement you'll never hear from anyone but me!... "Words stored in your Storage Units!")

WORDS TO PAY ATTENTION TO...MY **BELIEF WORDS** are the same as... **MY 'ITS' & MY 'TAG ALONGS'**

What is **TAKING UP SPACE IN MY STORAGE UNITS?**

- MY Belief Words... Are you understanding how WORDS/STATEMENTS MADE TO or ABOUT YOU, coming from others, can soon become your Belief Words – Positive and the negative words – and how huge a part these WORDS can play in your life? Do these Belief Words cause you to visualize yourself in a certain way? Yes! It's the application that you allow into your spirit, into your Belief-System.

- My 'ITS'... You have read in past Chapters about our 'ITS' – are words or statements someone has said to us, or about us, that you have now taken into your Belief System, your brain & heart, as the truth about yourself. Your 'ITS' are now your Belief Words ... saving them as TRUTH words about yourself. BELIEVING "IT," whatever IT is, to be the truth about ourselves is not necessarily always the TRUTH! RIGHT?

- My TAG ALONGS... Is what I like to call them. Why? Because, they-go-everywhere-we-go! When we walk through any door into any room, sitting on a sofa, and even if we're walking out in an open field, our Belief Words TAG-ALONG with us!

- My STORAGE UNITS... Every part of your body has a specified purpose of function, from the top of your head to the bottom of your feet. However, there are two purposes in your body that you cannot live without, that keeps you as a functional being. Are you ready to learn what they are? They are your BRAIN and HEART! Our BRAIN is one unit that obtains words through our ears or eyes and our minds hang onto them, and then take them to HEART as belief.

Each one of us, sooner instead of later, needs to examine our stored-up Belief Words, aka... our 'ITS', our 'TAG-ALONGS' and determine if they are false and give no value into our Journey-Walk – or if they are positive and add blessings to our walk. And, determine if you have made a permanent decision to keep them as your Belief Words! Ladies, understand what is TAKING UP SPACE IN YOUR STORAGE UNITS... your brain and heart!

Shouldn't we be asking ourselves.... **"Which do I want to store the most in my storage units, positive or negative beliefs?"**

Are you understanding how big a part 'WORDS of STATEMENTS' coming from others can soon become our Belief Words and how huge a part these words can play in our lives? Ladies, what do you store within your mind and heart? Which do you hang on to most in your thoughts? The Positive or Negative Words of Statements?

What takes up the most room in your deep-down Heart Beliefs, the positives or negatives?

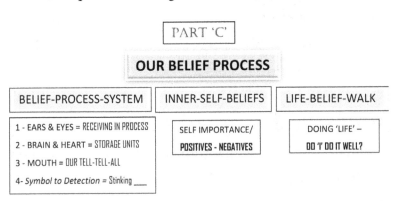

PART 'C'

OUR BELIEF PROCESS

BELIEF-PROCESS-SYSTEM	INNER-SELF-BELIEFS	LIFE-BELIEF-WALK
1 - EARS & EYES = RECEIVING IN PROCESS 2 - BRAIN & HEART = STORAGE UNITS 3 - MOUTH = OUR TELL-TELL-ALL 4- *Symbol to Detection* = Stinking ___	SELF IMPORTANCE/ POSITIVES - NEGATIVES	DOING 'LIFE' – DO 'I' DO IT WELL?

OUR BELIEF-PROCESS... This is probably the most important of these three Parts in the outline. Not that the other two are not important, because they are of great importance. But, PART THREE should really speak to you! While reading the statements below, look back at the top of the page to the diagram boxes. Did you know we were born with a Processing System within our bodies? Are you shocked? Yes, we have a Belief Processing System that processes our thoughts and turns them into our Beliefs.

Let's look into each one – one at a time... **BELIEF-PROCESS SYSTEM**... (Look in the box diagram, directly under BELIEF-

PROCESS-SYSTEM.) It's made up of three different parts of our bodies! It is the 'method' which Processes the Positive and/or Negative Beliefs into our Belief-System.

EARS & EYES = RECEIVING IN PROCESS ... How do we receive words of positivity or negativism? We either hear them with our ears or read them with our eyes, as a statement someone has said about us. And, then those 'Words of Statements' go into our Storage Units.

BRAIN & HEART = STORAGE UNITS ... Upon seeing it with our eyes or hearing it with our ears, the words are now within our brain. As you've already learned, we can allow these words to remain in our brain long enough so that they become beliefs and are now stored in our hearts, where they remain as Belief Words. We are believing it's the truth about us.

MOUTH = OUR TELL-TELL-ALL ... What happens then? At any point we use these 'WORDS of STATEMENTS' to tell others how we see ourselves. Most of the time... we don't even realize we're doing it. Not that we're repeating what that person had said about us. But, in the time these words have settled into our Hearts, they show others how we feel about ourselves.

For example, if you have been belittled, slandered by someone, and you take it in as the truth - that's now how you see yourself.

How, then, do you pass on your belief to others to recognize what you believe in yourself? Through your mouth! And, usually not in a Positive way. Or, if you have been encouraged by someone with positive Words of Statements, you have a good feeling and attitude. And, it seems to automatedly spread to others, through your mouth. This is why I call this part... OUR TELL-TELL ALL! Our emotions, our feelings and beliefs that are in our Belief-System get passed on to others.

SYMBOL to DETECTION = STINKING-THINKING

... This pretty well explains itself. When we hear others, or ourselves, speaking Negativism about us in general, that is a SYMBOL to DETECTION that there's something within our BELIEF-SYSTEM, which needs adjusting or let go of completely! STINKING THINKING takes us where, Ladies? NO WHERE FAST!! NO WHERE POSITIVE!!

Look back to our diagram page in PART C – Second Box...
I~N~N~E~R SELF-BELIEFS

SELF IMPORTANCE / POSITIVES – NEGITIVES

How importantly do we take ourselves? Depends on how much we have within us, POSITIVE or NEGATIVE BELIEFS, and how much time we spend in each Belief.

Third Box on the diagram page...

LIFE-BELIEF-WALK: DOING 'LIFE' – DO I DO IT WELL?

Ladies, only you can answer that question. Our Bible verse for this Chapter is found in **Romans 7:22... "For in my I~N~N~E~R being (self) I delight in GOD ..."** Where is our I~N~N~E~R BEING? They are the areas of which GOD created within us... our BRAINS (MINDS), our HEARTS(SOULS) and our EARS and MOUTHS! And, our mindful and spoken BELIEFS!

Ladies, how well is your I~N~N~E~R BEING in your walk with GOD? How well is your Journey-Walk among people? How well is your I~N~N~E~R BEING?

LET'S CARRY THIS THOUGHT WITH US...

Our real BEAUTY comes from two places within our body, plus two from an activity that is activated from the first two. These four areas within our bodies are... Our BRAINS/MINDS, Our HEARTS, Our VOICES and Our ACTIONS are the activities that are activated from #1 (Brain) and #2 (Heart). CONCLUSION: The first 2 are coming from our I~N~N~E~R Beliefs, our MINDS & HEARTS; and 3-4,

our VOICES & ACTIONS are the activity RESULTS from
the first two!

Chapter Six Reflections

Within those 5 simple words – ACCEPTANCE, CONVINCED, CERTAINTY in CONFIDENCE, we take Ownership in Words as being the Truth, good and bad, in what others have said to us or about us! They are now known as our BELIEF WORDS!

What are some of the 'Words of Statements' I've taken into my BELIEF-SYSTEM that have been a blessing and proven to be beneficial to me?

Give an example of one of your NEGATIVE BELIEF WORDS.

Give an example of one of your POSITIVE BELIEF WORDS.

Give three examples each that you know are taking up useful space in BELIEF-SYSTEM.

NOTE TAKING SPACE

Chapter Seven

THE 7 PRINCIPLES OF SELF-PRINCIPLE #1 – **SELF-CONCEPT**

"For in my INNER being, I delight in GOD ..."
Romans 7:22 (NIV)

According to the dictionary, Self-Concept is...the idea, or mental image, one has of oneself (Self-Concept, 2020)

Self-Concept according to CJ is: How we see ourselves overall. What we truly believe about ourselves as a Human being, as a Lady, and most importantly, as a Child of GOD, and... WHO and WHAT we desire to become! Each of us needs to explore what we truly believe about OUR-SELF from the INSIDE – OUT, and... Know what our main purpose is each day and each minute of our lives! Because, in order to improve ourselves, we first must know SELF. We need to know what we believe and SEE within ourselves, the Positives and the Negatives!

WE ARE the OVERSEER of OUR OWN BELIEFS!

This Chapter is in reference to your Self-Concept, which is how you personally see your I~N~N~E~R BEAUTY. Knowing your I~N~N~E~R-SELF is knowing what is true and false in your I~N~N~E~R BELIEFS, and what is and is not beneficial to your life. And, it may require a high level of self- examination regularly. Because, a belief that may not have been within your Belief-system last month may be there today.

To know and understand how important your I~N~N~E~R BEAUTY is to your present existence, is to know what you have discovered helpful to hang onto from your past, while knowing what you've currently accomplished and deposited into your future Journey-Walks that raises your Self-WORTH to a higher level of importance for yourself. You are the overseer of your own beliefs, Ladies.

Some people spend their entire lives building themselves a unique facade 'identity' on how they want others to see them. But yet, on the inside, their I~N~N~E~R Beliefs are slightly or totally different. This is why it's important to do some research into our I~N~N~E~R-SELF frequently. If you're not connected with who you truly are vs. who you can be, you're probably just living your life for others and missing

95

out on so many blessings GOD has for YOU! Ladies, you are the overseer of your Self-Concept. If not, you should be! No one else should live within your brain and heart. No one else should be allowed to control your thoughts, beliefs and dreams.

Throughout the pages of the Bible it speaks of our I~N~N~E~R SELF in reference to...

1. **Having CHRIST in our Hearts...** That's the most important. "**... you were washed, you were sanctified, you were justified in the name of the LORD JESUS CHRIST and by the Spirit of our GOD**" **1 Corinthians 6:11 (NIV)**. When we have been washed in the Blood of JESUS CHRIST, we are made a new person in HIM, therefore, a NEW PERSON to ourselves and to others! When we have CHRIST in our Hearts, we have been washed, sanctified, justified by JESUS CHRIST and by the Spirit of GOD! If that doesn't excite your thoughts and Hearts and give you a Hallelujah Voice to sing HIS praises, I don't know what will!

2. As a child of GOD"**...we are GOD's children**" **Romans 8:16 (NIV)**. We have a FATHER who loves us, protects us and blesses us in so many ways that we cannot count them all! Ladies... sing with

your Hallelujah Voice... "AMEN! GOD loves HIS children!"

3. As a Lady... **"He created mankind in HIS own image"
   Genesis 1:26.** GOD created us to LOVE, PROTECT
   our love, and we were made to be a BLESSING to all
   just the way our GOD is to us!

4. Believing What Can Be Accomplished... **"I can
   do all things through HIM who strengthens and
   empowers me..." Philippians 4:13 (NIV)** We can
   do ALL things through GOD! Here again, sing HIS
   Hallelujah Praises!

Ladies, sing this song with me, using your own melody...

"I have been washed, sanctified, and justified by JESUS
CHRIST and by the Spirit of GOD, because I am a child
of HIS. Created in HIS likeness, I can do all things through
GOD who strengthens and empowers me... AMEN –
AMEN– AMEN!"

Singing this song helps us memorize the verses and truth-
filled statements above, so we can share them with others
who may need to know how and what they could be through
CHRIST JESUS.

WE HAVE CHOICES!

Our Self-Concept shapes our everyday life. It creates and determines the kind of life we choose to live. Whether we make right or wrong choices, we still have to live within our CHOICES. This is why it is so important we go to GOD first.

VISUALIZE THIS... You hear or read words someone is saying to you with your EARS or EYES and it then enters into your MINDS/BRAINS, where it's going to dwell for a period of time.

Then there will be one of four choices that will be made by YOU personally...

- KEEP THEM... You keep holding onto those words in your THOUGHTS/BRAINS to determine if they are words of truth or false, or...
- BLOCK THEM... You decide they are 'Words of Destruction,' so you block them and refuse to believe them before they settle into your HEART! Or, you...
- WELCOME THEM... If they are 'Words of TRUE CONFIDENCE and ENCOURAGEMENT,' you should welcome them into your Heart to dwell among the best of your POSITIVE BELIEFS. And, keep them fresh in your mind, so they can be brought forth in time of need for you personally or to help others.

Then there's another point to make here. What if you...

- CONTINUE TO HOLD ONTO OLD NEGA-
TIVE BELIEFS THROUGHOUT LIFE... That's
a choice you need to determine the outcome conse-
quences. We all know what happens when Words of
Destruction, Words of Negativity settle in our Hearts,
don't we? We never seem to be able to let go of them.
Here again, this is where we need GOD. Now, if they
are bringing optimistic words and thoughts into our
beliefs and attitudes... lets welcome them.

Ladies, WE HAVE CHOICES, but for many reasons some
of us tend to forget to NOT ALLOW the negatives into
our Belief-System to begin with. If you live on the negative
side of the street in life, you are not only putting yourself in
the trenches, maybe even into a bottomless pit of negativism,
but you're living an example that others see and possibly will
follow as well. Do you really want this to happen? What does
all this do to your everyday functioning? It will especially
have an influence to all that are within your acquaintance
circle, and possibly to strangers.

Ladies, most people won't see you any differently than how
you see yourself!

AFFIRMATION of TRUTH

Self-Concept is a collection of Beliefs about oneself. Generally, Self-Concept embodies the answer to "Who am I?" (Self-Concept, 2020) Our Self-Concept, the Positive, the Good, the Bad and the Ugly, is who and what we consciously and subconsciously think we are, what we believe our abilities are, and how we see that our future will be. It's who we perceive we are as a person, a wife or girlfriend, mother, employee, co-worker or employer, friend, etc., etc.

Let's go much deeper with discovering which is the strongest in our Beliefs of our SELF... the Negatives or the Positives. We'll begin with the negatives and get them out of the way first...

THE NEGATIVES IN OUR LIVES: SOMEONE ELSE LEADS YOU

Sometimes, Self-Concept is what we say about ourselves that is not necessarily accurate or is totally wrong. Why? For one reason, as was my story for many years, we've been led to believe what someone else thinks about us is the truth. Therefore, we take it to Heart that this is who we are. We take it as an... Affirmation of Truth.

You may have lived as I did, growing up and the first several years as an adult, with a highly inaccurate definition of what

I was capable of accomplishing or could become. Therefore, I lived most of my life in a lie, living someone else's plans for me. They had no idea who I truly was or what I could become, because they were too busy molding me into their clay pot, which, by the way, finally cracked! Instead of teaching me and allowing my heavenly FATHER to be my 'Potter' and allowing me to be HIS clay, I was a messy clay pot of their molding. I was never told I could do all things through GOD who loves me when it was in HIS plan and will.

You might say I was a victim of circumstances. Well, to that statement I would say, as a child, and then a teenager, I had no choice, I was a victim. However, I will admit, for the most part, thereafter, I placed myself in that victim seat by my own choosing (wrong choices). I made many mistakes when I was single, because as a young adult I felt like I had no choice... until I finally learned later in life... I DID have a choice.

It's true, we aren't always responsible for some of the circumstances in which we find ourselves. However, we are responsible for the way we respond to them and what we choose to do to get out of certain situations. We can give over to the crisis and keep falling deeper in the bottomless pit. Or, we can look to our Sovereign LORD who can place everything under control, if we would only ALLOW HIM to do so. HE can show us a way out of the bottomless pit and give us new life. Then, HE can use our experiences for our ultimate good by transforming us to the image of CHRIST as it says in **2 Corinthians 3:18… "…we are being transformed into HIS likeness with ever-increasing glory, which comes from the LORD, who is the SPIRIT" (NIVSB)** Ladies, this is where GOD has brought me… using me to help other Ladies, who may be where I used to be…in the bottomless pit!

Yes, Self-CONCEPT can be defined as an all comprehensive awareness of yourself in a negative way. Your PAST may have now moved up into your PRESENT. Carrying baggage from the PAST can take you nowhere, because your beliefs never change, your CONCEPT of whom you'd rather be in life is buried in those 'old-suitcases-of-your-past-beliefs, so therefore, nothing ever changes in your BELIEFS!

When I taught classes from my material I have written called, 'Having the Confidence Walk and Posture In CHRIST,' I would have an old suitcase packed with books. The suitcase was passed around the classroom to help all the Ladies in the room understand Self-Concept. Negative thoughts are extremely heavy, they weigh on us so much. The big, old, heavy suitcase in their laps for a period of time helped them understand how much of a burden their negative thoughts could be on their Self-Concept and how awkward it is to work around them. It also allowed them to see how light things were without the heavy junk, weighing them down!

FINALLY, LET'S TALK ABOUT.... THE POSITIVES

We've established that our Self-Concept is generally thought of as an awareness of our deep personal mind and heart beliefs. And, isn't it satisfying when the awareness is of our own achievements, we have accomplished from life experiences that we're proud to claim? Ladies, there's nothing wrong with being proud of ourselves when we have worked so hard to achieve a goal... we should be proud! AMEN? AMEN!!

You may have withstood the hardships and battles that arose in your life which had the intent to belittle and tear you down. But, you remained strong in your Self-Belief and with GOD's help and guidance, you overcame and conquered all things thrown your way in order – to – reach – your –goals! And, you did just that! PRAISE GOD!

Does it make a difference in your life as to which side of the street you live and stay on... the negative side or the positive side? I think we're all in agreement to which side we prefer, so if you're not already on the positive side of the street right now.... Hurry up and get yourself moved over there. And as you're moving be sure to throw away those old suitcases of junky negative beliefs! It's so much prettier and fulfilling on the positive side of life! KEEP READING this BOOK and asking GOD to show you the way!

Let's look at some proven facts as to how Self-Concept can affect us daily and long term. Did you know that...

- How we feel and what we see in ourselves affects virtually every aspect of our existence, from the way we function... at work, in relationships, with our family and friends, as an employee or employer, and it could affect our health in some ways.

- Almost, I say almost every single psychological problem people have is traceable to a poor Self-Concept, that is... one's self-imaging of oneself. That's scary! Isn't it?

- Sometimes Self-Concept is what we say about ourselves that is not necessarily accurate. Why? We have been led to believe that what other people think about us is the truth!

- Then, we take it as our affirmation to the truth, of which, isn't the truth in GOD's plans! Now that's sad, but I was once one of those believers.

- If we see ourselves as a fixed entity, never changing, then any SELF-change we try to do could become threatening and an anxiety-producing action.

We saturate our MINDS with so much of these negatives that our hearts begin believing what we tell it.

WHO DO WE ALLOW TO MOLD US? Who do we allow to control our Beliefs? (What is your first thought when you read each point below.) It could be:

- People in our past or present
- A family member
- Someone we think of as a friend
- A teacher
- A neighbor
- Someone we may associate with at work
- A stranger

Could some of these be people you may need to distance yourself from now? What molds your Self-Concept...

- Your lifestyle – WHY?
- Circumstances – WHAT?
- Abuse from the past or present – WHO?
- A time of disappointment – WHEN?
- Positive and Happy times – WHEN?
- Your Walk with GOD – WHERE?
- Negative and Positive thoughts and beliefs – FROM WHO or WHAT?

All, some or none, of the points listed above can tear you down or build you up! I'm going for 'UP' myself, instead of DOWN! How about you? Because, viewing ourselves with negative Self-Labels can produce dysfunctional thoughts, hurt feelings, bad habits and more disruptive beliefs. All these can undermine success in our careers, our relationships and our everyday duties and responsibilities.

WHAT DOES GOD DESIRE FROM US?

Our Heavenly FATHER wants us to develop our I~N~N~E~R-SELF into more of HIS likeness and remember as I've told you before... HIS likeness is AWAYS ON the POSITIVE SIDE! HE's right here with each one of us to help us reach our GOALS – when our plans are lined up with HIS plans.

LADIES, PAY CLOSE ATTENTION TO THIS...Isn't it ironic that when we talk about setting our "GOALS" to accomplish something Positive and then DO IT, our minds and hearts are always in the frame of being positive? We never refer to setting goals in a negative frame of mind, unless it's planned to be negative, and by the way, that's not a GOAL! What does that say to you? Think about it a few minutes.

~⁓∾⊙⌒

UNAWARE OF PASSING THE MESSAGE ONWARD

A MUST READ for ALL MOTHERS AND GRANDMOTHERS, AUNTS and Others

When you voice your negative beliefs and feelings before children, teenagers, and even younger adults, what are you saying to them? With having negative beliefs about yourself, what kind of message does this send to young girls and young Ladies, and even young boys? Your voice is saying that it's okay for them to believe negative junk about themselves, because they hear of your negative beliefs.

Do you realize, we are held responsible for being role models? Believe me, they're listening, and they are learning, whether you think they are or not. If they see you with such a low self-image of yourself, being a grown woman, what do they carry in their minds throughout their lifetime? One more thought... what do they have to look forward to in finding their own Self-Worth?

If you are a negative belief person, do you want these young girls and young Ladies to have what you have...a low value of themselves? Do you want them seeing or hearing all about your baggage? Their eyes are always watching. Their ears are always turned on, whether you think they are or not. They may be someone kin to you, or your friend's daughter or some young lady you work with. You never know who may be watching and hearing you.

Or, it could be an adult Lady who is struggling with her own Self-Worth and have been hurt or looked down upon and is in need of someone to speak POSITIVE words into her life. Do you get it? So, what are they seeing? What are these young girls and grown Ladies hearing from your mouth that gives them a message of Self- IMPORTANCE? Anything? Anything at all?

Ladies, be extra careful what you voice before them. Turn the knob totally off on negative statements and beliefs in front of children and young people, and preferably all people. This is one of those things I told you at the beginning of the book you wouldn't want to hear. However, dwell on that for a moment and determine what example you may be setting!

First, we need to realize and understand what all the junk, and all the Negatives are in our own lives – in our Belief-System – in order to make changes in our Self-Concept! We must rid ourselves of all the negatives, because our beliefs are being pasted on to the younger generations!

LADIES, LET'S DO OUR PART and KEEP THE GOOD AND RID OURSELVES OF THE BAD!

Because, remember this... we are the ones who have to live inside our bodies, while we're here on this earth. So, therefore, there is a great need to understand ourselves, no matter how ugly or how unworthy we think we are at the time. I promise, the two words in that last sentence... 'ugly and unworthy' will no longer be existing in your beliefs, when you have a change in your BELIEF-SYSTEM! If they do still exist in your beliefs, you need to re-read this book again, and pray more.

I'll leave this on a POSITIVE thought...

The memories you have of the PAST, and the expectations you have of yourself for the FUTURE never should take the place of the POSITIVE awareness you need to have of yourself in the PRESENT. You should allow your NEGATIVES to remain in the PAST, and dwell less on the FUTURE until you take care of the PRESENT. And, then go forward with great potentials.
- A CJism

Where do we want to continue our Journey-Walk? In the past? Sorry, you don't have any control over your past – you no longer live there! In the future? Sorry, no control there either, Ladies....or right now in the PRESENT – Where you do have control over what you take into your Belief-System?

Summing It Up... What is Self-Concept? It's the self-belief of ones-self. How we see ourselves affects every aspect of our existence, from the way we function at work, at home with our family and friends, or people in general, while in the public eye.

LET'S CARRY THIS THOUGHT WITH US...

You can look forward to the FUTURE but take care of your BELIEFS right now in the PRESENT, so you can have something to look forward to as well! Ladies, Heal and Learn from the PAST, so that you can walk in the PRESENT with Self-Respect, Self-Love, Self-Motivation, and Self-Confidence, and LOOK FORWARD to a much improved and higher success of Self-Worth in YOUR FUTURE! Change the Present Self-Concept so that the future will be perceived as POSITIVE!

Ephesians 3:16... "I pray that out of HIS glorious riches HE may strengthen you with power through HIS spirit in your I~N~N~E~R being." (NIV)

YOUR MEMORY VERSE: **"But the LORD stood at my side, and gave me strength, so that through me the message might be fully proclaimed..." 2 Timothy 4:17 (NIV).**

How many times has the LORD stood by your side and gave you strength? More times than you'll ever know. Are you sharing the message? So that others may know and proclaim GOD in their lives?

Chapter Seven Reflections

Self-Concept – the idea or mental image one has of one's self. If you live on the negative side of the street of life, you are not only putting yourself in the trenches, maybe even into a bottomless pit of negativism. you're living an example that others see and possibly will follow as well. Carrying baggage from the PAST can take me nowhere, because my beliefs never change, my CONCEPT of whom I'd rather be in life is buried in those 'old-suitcases-of-our-past-beliefs' so therefore, NOTHING NEVER changes in my BELIEFS! I should allow my NEGATIVES to remain in the PAST and I shouldn't dwell on the FUTURE until I take care of the PRESENT.

I may need to realize and understand what all the junk is – all the Negative – that lives in my BELIEF-SYSTEM, in order to make changes in my Self-Concept. I must rid myself of all the negatives, because my BELIEFS could be pasted on to the younger generations; or someone hurting from others' hurtful words who may be listening to you!

Romans 8:37... "... in all things we are more than conquerors through HIM who loves us." (NIV)

Do I take the time to evaluate what I hear or read from words someone has said to or about me?

What determines if I KEEP THEM, BLOCK THEM or WELCOME THEM?

Why do I allow SOMEONE to take over my THOUGHTS and BELIEFS in a negative way?

There is nothing wrong about being 'proud' of myself when I have worked hard to achieve my goals!" TRUE/ FALSE

Knowing what I know now, how would I describe Self-Concept?

Ladies, maybe there's a need within you to be renewed or even changed. But, how are you going to know HOW to change your 'SELF' from bad habits, if you don't ask GOD to reveal them all to you? WHEN will you learn HOW GOD DESIGNED you to be, if you don't examine your I~N~N~E~R present-thoughts-and-beliefs? Most likely, never! This may be the problem as well.

NOTE TAKING SPACE

Chapter Eight

PRINCIPLE #2 – **SELF-RESPECT**

According to the dictionary, Self-Respect is... "A regard for the dignity of one's character" (Self-Respect, 2020a), "Pride and Confidence in oneself; a feeling that one is behaving with honor and dignity "(Self-Respect, 2020b) and... "Believing that you are good and worthy of being treated well" (Self-Respect, 2020c).

Now for some Self-Respect according to CJ... To hold ourselves up to Having an UNCONDITIONAL POSITIVE REGARD for ourselves.

1 Timothy 3:11... "In the same way, the women are to be 'worthy of respect'..."

Ladies, are you modeling yourselves in accordance to this verse?

RESPECTING OURSELVES AS A BEAUTIFUL LADY and AS A CHILD OF THE KING... DO YOU THINK THIS IS SOMETHING OUR HEAVENLY FATHER DEEPLY DESIRES FROM US? Of course, HE does. After all, HE was the ONE who breathed LIFE into us. So, why wouldn't HE love to see us RESPECT what HE has created within us!!

"Whoever gives heed to instruction will prosper and blessed is the one who trusts in the LORD."
Proverbs 16:20 (NIV)

This book was designed to introduce to you the BEAUTY that is within you. The beauty of your mind and Heart, and yes, the beauty of your body. It is all the beauty of GOD 's creation and gifts to you. The image of your deeper beliefs of yourself will come from within you and will sooner, if not later, be seen by others. And, hopefully the message received will be beautiful!

Ladies, GOD already knows your beauty and your potential. Remember...HE was the ONE who created you. There's a possibility HE has brought you to this book to help you realize what HE created within you that needs to be utilized by you at this time in life (utilize – ACTION – needs to happen) and continuing on throughout your entire life Journey-Walk.

GOD already knows your WORTH. Remember, HE was the first one to love you. HE knew you before your birth HE knew you in your mother's womb, and HE knows HIS plan for you. HIS love and admiration for you will always be greater than your own opinion of yourself could ever be. Don't you just love this verse? **"...your INNER self, the unfading beauty... which is of great worth in GOD's sight." 1 Peter 3:4 (NIV).**

In order to see and know HIS love to the fullest extent, to know HIS calling for your life, and to realize the I~N~N~E~R BEAUTY that is within you, which should be lived as a reflection of GOD, you must first break the negative chains that holds you captive! We all have to get out of that confined-old-smelly-suitcase, so we can see and know HIS plans for our lives. Ladies, we have to understand that becoming self-accepting of GOD'S plans for us means to have a desire to change and accept the fact that we may have to do so in order to improve our I~N~N~E~R BEAUTY, while surrounding ourselves with others whose desires and goals are the same.

The SEVEN SELF-ACCEPTANCE ACTIONS

Self-Acceptance is something YOU do. It's an active process that involves...

- A willingness of accepting the things you like and love about yourself, rather than denying them.
- Acknowledging and then changing the things you wish we were not.
- Admitting the Beliefs and Actions you desire to change can only come to pass with...
- Your readiness to let go of them, and...
- Giving over to GOD the power to change them, then you will...
- Realize your true worth. It all begins with YOU! YOU must have the...
- Willingness to let go and begin with a new BELIEF in yourself.

HOW MUCH DO I RESPECT MY OWN BEING?

Making This PERSONAL. Starting with... Respecting my relationship with GOD. Then to further my own good... personally RESPECTING my MIND, my HEART, and my VALUES. And, the least pleasant, which I don't like to talk about, is...respecting my body. What do I allow into my mind and heart that's disrespectful to my own being? Now that's a question I really need to give some thought to as well. I'll ask myself again... What do I allow into my MIND, HEART and BODY that's disrespectful to my own being and has an influence in my present and future Journey-Walk (my everyday walk through life)?

PERSONALLY, answer these following questions...

- What do I allow into my MIND & HEART that's DISRESPECTFUL to my own being?
- Do I RESPECT myself enough not to allow others to hurt or destroy my Positive I~N~N~E~R thoughts and beliefs about myself?
- Should I be filtering out the negative thoughts that may be trying to enter into my BRAIN? Because, once in my BRAIN, it won't take long for 'Words of Destruction' to enter into the core of my HEART. And, then it's hard, on many different levels, to rid myself of the Negatives.
- How much RESPECT do I give myself overall? NONE/ LITTLE / LOTS / DEPENDS on what's happened.
- How do I filter out the Negatives?
- Seriously, how much RESPECT do we give ourselves overall?

RESPECTING ourselves is another image GOD desires us to have for ourselves.

IN RESPECT FOR ONE'S SELF-RESPECT

Does our ATTITUDE, our MINDSET, have anything to do with our Self-Respect? "We must have a Positive ATTITUDE in order to have a Positive MINDSET, which builds up our Self-Respect!" (Last sentence a quote from my husband, David. He's been listening to my talks.)

Ladies, how about investing some of your precious time into building a new and positive image of yourself? Have you ever thought about how it could actually change your attitude throughout your entire Journey-Walk? It could be the best 'time' you may ever spend, because you'll soon see upon changes, the Negativism will not hold a place in your life, your thoughts, your hearts or your world. How does that sound to you?

If you have read, or heard, of some of my past history, I finally got to a place in my life where I was determined to turn those horrible experiences I lived through, into learning lessons to never do again or place myself in situations that would bring evil into my life. And, my life now has brought me much more happiness and rewards!

You may say, "But, that's you. GOD can't do in me what HE's done in you!" I will answer you back by saying... "YES HE CAN, and then some, if need be!" HE has a plan for each and every one of us. We just have to get to the place in our lives where we will LISTEN and OBEY HIM. I can testify to that! If we don't RESPECT ourselves, how can we expect others to respect us?

RESPECTING ourselves is what brings to the surface our INTEGRITY and our IDENTITY that'll give us the ABILITY to do anything we set out to do. Of course, if it is within GOD's plans for you and with HIS help and guidance.

So far, so good, Ladies? Are you beginning to see the picture here? This was the purpose of writing this book, especially for those of you who may need some help in certain areas and better understanding that you are rated highly with WORTH in GOD 's eyes and Heart! This is why this book's title speaks to so many Ladies, because, do we not all want to be... 'THE CONFIDENT LADY OF PURPOSE'?

Ladies, what is your PURPOSE here on this earth? You won't truly know GOD'S entire PURPOSE for your life, until you learn and understand who HE has created YOU to be... to the fullest!

Let's look at this... What does Self-Respect GIVE US PERSONALLY? INTEGRITY and our IDENTITY, that'll give us the ABILITY to do anything we set out to do.

2 Corinthians 5:5 (NIV)... "Now the ONE who has fashioned us for this very purpose is GOD, who has given us the SPIRIT as a deposit, guaranteeing what is to come." So, what is to come in your life, Ladies?

TO CHANGE or NOT TO CHANGE –
THAT IS the QUESTION!

If I choose to not ask GOD for removal of all my Junky-Beliefs
and garbage that I have placed within my Belief-System, I am
the one who made the choice not to change. I am the one who
will continue to carry all the baggage around with me. I am
the one who keeps myself in my own bondage. I am the one who
broke the TRUST! Now, it's time to mend and begin believing
in myself again (or maybe for the first time) and ask GOD for
guidance! - A CJism

Give some thought to this statement... Not being fully aware
of SELF is similar to being separated from an identity of SELF.
So, say these words to yourself:

- 'I' must give 'MYSELF' the permission to change
  things that need changing
- 'I' must RESPECT 'MYSELF' by not allowing people
  to disrespect 'ME'
- 'I' must be careful what 'I' say about myself in front of
  others
- 'I' must START RESPECTING 'MY' own MIND,
  HEART and BODY!

What Is RESPECT for SELF? ... Trusting in myself and
holding myself up with Statements of Positive Assessments,

which gives me Unconditional Positive Regard into my new Identity as a Lady and as a Child of CHRIST JESUS!!

A LIGHT BEFORE OTHERS...

"Do nothing out of selfish ambition or vain concept, but in humility consider others better than yourself. Each of you should look not only to your own interest, but also to the interests of others. In your relationships with one another, have the same mindset as JESUS CHRIST."
Philippians 2:3-5 (NIV)

Self-RESPECT basically means... Holding yourself up with a true statement of Positive visual statements of yourself as in our regard to your identity! Another words... Let it be known, that others may see, that you regard yourself with high RESPECT! Be the LIGHT in their dis-belief! **"... have the same mindset as JESUS CHRIST."**

Ladies, do you need to make a CHANGE? Do you need to give yourself permission to CHANGE? Permission meaning... giving your best efforts to change what needs to be changed in your thoughts and beliefs.

If we have RESPECT for ourselves, it will be a 'light' before others to the degree that what is seen within us will naturally demand RESPECT from others without having to do much more than being ourselves! - A CJism

All Actions start with a strong desire to bring something into existence (or do what you have to do to keep in existence). A personal example: Having a desire to write this Bible Study, I searched my I~N~N~E~R Beliefs to find whether or not I believed I could accomplish this desire I felt GOD calling me to do. I have been writing Bible studies for years to teach within my Ladies ministry, have even started a couple of novels hoping one day to see one or more on the shelves in book stores, but truthfully, deep down, never did I ever believe I would actually have any of my writings published. This book you're holding came from one of the Bible Studies series I have written and taught several times over the years.

I prayed, and prayed some more, knowing all along I didn't have a degree in English nor Writing nor Theology, but yet the desire was still strong because I knew it was a calling from GOD. I am not a Bible scholar by any means, but I'm always amazed when GOD leads me to the perfect verses and passages in the Bible for the topic I'm writing at that moment! I've since learned that having a strong DESIRE, and knowing without doubt it's a calling from GOD, can be as important as a degree when it's truly a message from GOD! And too, it helps when you have great, patient editors!

The devil tried everything to discourage me and to put roadblocks in my way to cause delays in me writing. But- I worship an ALL-MIGHTY-ALL-POWERFUL GOD that has more powers than that old devil ever thought about having!

Your desire to accomplish something most likely will not come to pass, unless it gives you value in the meaning of doing it. And, you cannot accomplish something to the full extent, unless you desire to accomplish it. There must be a match between what you would like to do, what you intend to do and what you actually do (Take ACTION). You must have a genuine effective ACTION in trying to accomplish it – whatever 'it' is.

WHAT WE GIVE OUT, COMES RIGHT BACK

TREATING PEOPLE WITH RESPECT helps us get along with each other. It also helps to avoid and resolve conflicts and create a Positive social environment. We need to see and understand that respectful behavior means treating others with RESPECT and politeness, while accepting personal differences. Why? Because, as we all know, everyone has a right to their own views, beliefs and theories, and we must accept that.

In most cases, RESPECT is given when received. Listen to what others have to say, and refrain from ridiculing, embarrassing or hurting someone. Launch a silent agreement that each of us have a role in creating a respectful relationship. You will then experience an inspiring RESPECT between you and other(s), whether it's just one-on-one with someone, in a small group or among others in a large crowd. If RESPECT continues to not be seen between you and another person, it may be time to then reevaluate the relationship between the two of you. Give some thought and prayer into the situation, and then listen to your Heart.

1 Corinthians 3:10 (NIV) ... "By the grace GOD has given me, I laid a foundation as a wise builder, and someone else is building on it."

Are you the kind of person others could build upon your Foundation of Beliefs? Show RESPECT and RESPECT will be returned!

RESPECTING OUR BODIES

I bet you thought this CHAPTER was going to be all about RESPECTING our bodies. How we take or do not take care of our bodies. What we should and should not feed into our bodies through our mouths, or the fact that we should be – exercising our bodies. Right? Well, to be honest with you, no, that's not the purpose of this Chapter. However, there are a few lines below that do mention a few facts...

RESPECTING OUR BODIES means... listening to our body and emotions continuously, then acting beyond a straight-line judgement to achieve our goals. There are hundreds and hundreds of books you can read, programs you can attend, personal trainers and online videos you can listen to that will help you in this area. My only encouragement here is to understand deeply and remember these three questions...

- **Are not our bodies GOD'S temple? 1 Corinthians 6:19**
- **"Do you not know that your bodies are members of CHRIST HIMSELF?" 1 Corinthians 6:15a**
- Can I make a lasting promise to give my BODY, SOUL and LIFE over to GOD and obey HIS guidance?

Ephesians 4:24 (NIV) "... and to put on the new self, created to be like GOD in true righteousness and holiness."

OVERVIEW WITH POSITIVE BELIEFS

WHAT IS 'MY' PERSONAL CONCEPT of 'MY' SELF-RESPECT? Should it be MORE as in the following:

- I now have the knowledge and ability to treat myself with unconditional Positive RESPECT!

- This gives more integrity into my I~N~N~E~R SELF, because of my new attitude toward my new identity as a LADY, and as a CHILD of JESUS CHRIST, which I value and honor!

- I am in contact with myself. So, therefore, I'm trusting in myself, and holding myself up with high levels of 'Statements of Positive Assessments!'

- TRUSTWORTHINESS is the basis of all good relationships and cornerstone of good CHARACTER.

- And, I will, from this point on, be more trustworthy, because... TRUSTWORTHY PEOPLE keep their promises, because they are honest and reliable!

LET'S CARRY THIS THOUGHT WITH US...

Ladies, our mission and desires should be to become The LADY of the 6 Es... Extraordinary Ladies, Exploring Our Self-Images, Educating Our Minds, Enriching Our Hearts, Encouraging Our Souls and Expanding Our Self-Worth...
all through JESUS CHRIST! Yes, this should be our ongoing goal, our mission and our purpose in life. And, this will E-maze everyone in our life circle! (Last sentence is from my husband, David.)

Above all else, guard your Heart, for everything you do flows from it. Give careful thought to the paths for your feet and be steadfast in all your ways." Proverbs 4:24-26 (Paraphrased)

In order to see and know GOD's love to the full extent, to know HIS calling for my life, and to realize the I~N~N~E~R BEAUTY that is within me, which should be lived as a reflection of GOD, I must first break the negative chains that hold me captive! In regard to your identity that others may see, that you regard yourself with high RESPECT!

Why can't we have an unconditional Positive RESPECT for the attitude we have about ourselves? If we could learn to RESPECT ourselves as we RESPECT others, maybe we could relax a bit and not worry so much about what we feel we are not but wished to be. We could then develop good judgment about our VALUES, HONOR, INTEGRITY and ABILITY.

"Above all else, guard your Heart, for everything you do flows from it. – Give careful thought to the paths for your feet and be steadfast in all your ways." Proverbs 4:23 & 26

A PLEDGE of HONORING SELF

Self-Respect means to me that I'm now Trusting in ME, and holding ME up with Statements of Positive Assessments and treating ME with Unconditional Positive Regard! This gives ME a new Attitude toward MY new Identity as a LADY, and as a Follower of CHRIST JESUS!! BREAKING the chains from old Beliefs... easier said than done! WHY?

Think of three areas of my life that are missing RESPECT. This must be in my personal vision of myself ... not other people's opinion.....

- I value myself as ...
- I honor myself in ways of ...
- My integrity is worth more to me than...
- I view my ability to do more...

If I can respect my job, my boss(es), parents and grandparents, pastor, a dear friend, someone who is high profile, then why can't I RESPECT myself?

Why can't I hold myself up in UNCONDITIONAL POSITIVE REGARDS?

Name a couple, or more, of the above Actions you feel needs to take place in your personal beliefs that could make a huge difference in your life.

NOTE TAKING SPACE

Chapter Nine

PRINCIPLE #3 – **SELF-LOVE**

According to various dictionaries, Self-Love is... "Regard for one's own happiness or advantage. (Self-Love, 2020a), "A regard for one's own well-being and happiness" (Self-Love, 2020b) and "The instinct by which one's own Actions are directed to the promotion of one's own welfare or well-being" (Self-Love, 2020c).

Self-Love, according to CJ, an UNCONDITIONAL POSITIVE REGARD to ONE's OWN SELF. LOVE your Self in ways of protecting yourself from harmful and toxic negative beliefs. Protect yourself from 'words of destruction to Mind and Heart' from other people.

∼⦵∽

Someone once asked me why I placed the Self-Respect Chapter before the Self-Love Chapter. She thought we should LOVE ourselves first in order to RESPECT ourselves.

My response was... "Not that one is more important than the other but ... It's like in a relationship with the man you are in love with as an example. During the dating period with him, did the relationship begin with you seeing and experiencing all the things you respected in him. And, then, did the respect for him grow into you falling in love with him? What you saw and respected about him came first, before the falling-in love did; hopefully." Then my friend said she understood the answer to her question.

A relationship should begin with RESPECTING someone first. Why? Because real and lasting LOVE cannot have deep and long-lasting roots of growth without respecting one another for who and what they are as a person and what respect they give into the relationship. This is why I have placed Self-Respect before Self-Love in this book, as a scenario, because we must learn how to RESPECT ourselves from the inside out before we can truly understand ourselves as the Lady we were created to be by GOD. And, then comes the TRUE LOVE!

SINGLE LADIES; this is a short but 'to the point' message for you... If you're in a relationship with a man and you can't name at least seven Positive things that you respect about his character, actions/reactions and his personal, 'sincere' treatments toward you and to others, I'd suggest you truly question your relationship before going any further. Why? If you can't actually see that there's enough to RESPECT about the man, what's the guarantee there will be enough RESPECT there in order to LOVE and enjoy a lasting loving marriage? Ladies, I sincerely hope you will give plenty of deep thought into what you have just read in this paragraph now and in the future.

MOTHER'S OF YOUNG GIRLS; I would also highly suggest teaching your daughters this same guidance. First thing... If you don't already, begin TEACHING and SHOWING them the real meaning of RESPECT, beginning as a toddler and throughout their life growing up. They must know and understand the 'meaning,' before they can accept it as a Principle Action.

As a teenager, teach them to not 'settle' with just any young man. Teach them to be kind to everyone, but to know that being kind doesn't mean they should be spending lots of time with someone who cannot respect your child. Teach them to look for the RESPECT her pursuer may or may not be giving her, before she continues in the relationship. Teach her how to RESPECT HERSELF and to not allow any disrespect to come from anyone, much less her pursuer. And, Mothers, start teaching your sons at a young age the meaning of RESPECT toward young Girls and Ladies and toward others.

IT TAKES A LOT 'LESS ENERGY' to "LOVE" YOURSELF THAN IT DOES TO LIVE A NEGATIVE LIFESTYLE!

Why, you ask?

Because, the NEGATIVES that you build as your life's foundation will soon crumble, and they will. At some point they will fall down into roadblocks that you have to spend wasted time and energy removing throughout your life.
- A CJism

WHAT MAKES LADIES 'NOT' LOVE THEMSELVES?

I had asked a group of Ladies what the above statement meant to them and six replied. NOT LOVING yourself could be coming from numerous of beliefs, some being:

- No one has ever explained to you what Self-Love is really about
- You may be still carrying ANGER within you for different reasons
- Being belittled, hurt or taken advantage of by people far too many times
- Your physical appearance

Answers from my friends:

- Hanging onto 'scars' of the past way too long
- Feel broken inside, resulting in the loss of love for one's self
- We look for what we think others see in us instead of what JESUS sees
- Taking the blame of others' bad treatments
- The world messes with our head and teaches us what 'we should be' and we take it as truth instead of listening to GOD telling us 'who we really are.'
- The lack of respect and love from others or ourselves can plunge us so far into uncertainty that we cannot function.

Thank you, Ladies, for your insightful input in helping other Ladies to see where they too may be holding on to some things, they need to let go of as well.

A STATEMENT OF EGO ASSESSMENTS

To tell you the truth, I was a grown woman before I ever heard the word Self-Love. Then, I heard for many years that Self-Love was not something we should do, and for many years I believed that. I've stayed away from the belief that so many people usually associate Self-Love with, and that's a high level of self-centeredness. Some take having Self-Love as an arrogant way of thinking they're better than everyone else. No one else's thoughts, words or opinions are worthy of listening to, but theirs are worth it.

Here are a few definitions associated with egotistical behavior...

- Vain
- Boastful
- Selfish
- Highly Opinionated
- Indifferent to the well-being of others
- Believing to be worthier than those around them
- Only their viewpoints and beliefs matter
- Self-obsessed

I think you get the picture. Sooner or later they make clear what they truly believe about themselves in front of others or behind people's backs! And, it's very sad.

The most uncomfortable attitude to have towards ourselves is what we embrace as the TRUTH, no matter how untrue, how ugly or how bizarre it may be. Why? Because, this has been our comfort spot for so long and it has been a big part of our attitude. So, therefore, embracing a change in attitude that tells us otherwise ... 'we-no-can-do' ... UNTIL, we learn how to do it!

Has It Been All That Much of A Comfort Spot?

- Have you really been that comfortable believing all the negative things you have taken into your Belief-System (brain and heart), even though, deep down you know you need to change this or that negative belief?

- You know without a doubt that this change in attitude would be better and healthier for you and would take you to new and higher images of yourself, but maybe it's not a change you want to experience right now.

- You're comfortable where you are... miserable, but no goals to deal with or achieve, not deserving enough to change or believing you can't do it anyway.

- Even though you know certain changes would be worth so much more to you in the long run, you still hang onto your old untruths, your old baggage that keeps you in bondage. Why is that? Tell yourself the answer to that bold question!

Ladies, if you see yourself in any of the statements above, it makes me very sad. Because, I was once there myself, in all those statements. Continue on with this book and see where GOD leads you to make the needed changes in your life.

STATEMENTS of POSITIVE ASSESSMENTS

"You are the most influential person you'll ever talk to all day, please be careful with what you say to yourself." (Ziglar, 2018)

In this book, I'm NOT trying to take us back to the hippie era nor towards a New Age feminist movement, by no means, but rather to let you know what CHRIST JESUS has seen in you all along that maybe you had no idea what you could be enjoying within your own I~N~N~E~R BEAUTY. I want to help you see why Self-Love is one of the Six Principles that builds our Self-Worth! Self-Love, in most people's eyes, has the definition of, totally or mainly focused on one's own self-interest; in other words, engrossed in self; egotistical. So, with that said, let's learn what GOD has for us to know about what Self-Love is really all about...

Self-Love within our 'character values' is not classified as being self-centered but having LOVE for ourselves is another image GOD desires to see within us. If we say we LOVE someone, does this mean we are making a statement of 'Positive' assessments about them? If so, why is it so hard for us Ladies to have a statement of 'Positive' assessment about ourselves? Why – can't – we – LOVE – ourselves – at least on the same level as we LOVE others?

Self-Love is a statement of Positive assessments. I've read or heard it said to be ... 'a life journey of peacefulness' – 'a practice of good self-health-care towards a stress-free life.' When we love someone, do we not try and protect them from evil or labeling themselves with harmful judgements?

That's called LOVE! Right? Well, if we can LOVE that person enough to protect 'them,' why can't we do it for/to 'ourselves'? The key words are... PROTECTING OURSELVES from what could pull us down or going through life with negative labels hanging all over us!

Giving yourself Self-Love does not take away ALL your negative thoughts or beliefs. Remember, satan is never silent. There will always be times – but, the times will be less-and-less after we begin believing in ourselves – when we doubt ourselves of being worthy. But, staying strong in the belief that we are GOD's creation and HE IS the 'OVERSEER' of our life paths; we can continuously ask HIM to remove the negative thoughts from us and to protect us from the Negative evils.

Memorize this Scripture verse, and sing it in your mind, with your voice, when something negative is thrown at you or is trying to take over your thoughts and beliefs...

"Peace I have with You, LORD; not as the world gives me,
but as the Peace You give to me... I will not let my Heart
to be troubled nor afraid, for You are with me."

John 14:27 (paraphrased to sing)

POWERFUL PERSONAL FULFILLING PATH to
SELF-LOVE

Upon gathering my thoughts from how far I have come from
my past – to where I am today, I've put together this Powerful
Personal Fulfilling Path to Self-Love. Say it in your voice as
you are reading it to become personal in your beliefs.

"I have learned that if I would just:

- LOVE myself enough to Protect Self from the 4 A's...
  Anxiety, Anger, Annoyance and Adversity, and
- Practice MORE Self-KINDNESS and Self-
  COMPASSION, to
- GIVE myself Self-FORGIVENESS for my own
  mistakes,
- Identify WHY I'm having to do so in the first place,
  and
- Make AMENDs with myself and then
- Let it GO and GIVE myself
- TIME to myself to read and meditate on GOD's
  WORD, so I can be

- RELEASED from being stressful, and then I will
- LEARN more of how much GOD's LOVE can HEAL, REMOVE OLD BAGGAGE and BRING IN NEW LIFE into my LIFE!
- Because, when I ONLY see the dark thick clouds above me in life I see no rays of SUNSHINE!
- SO, I'm going to LET the 'SON OF GOD' SHINE IN MY LIFE FROM THIS POINT ON!!!"

For when I do, I will have a much more peaceful and fulfilling life with myself, that will spill over into my marriage, with family and friends, all people, things in general. And, I will have more time to spend loving what GOD is bringing forth in my life, along with ALL the blessings HE'S placing in my Journey-Walk!

Ladies, Self-LOVE is not a selfish action, it's a POSITIVE ACTION – a movement (ACTUALLY MOVING) toward experiencing a more enriching way to live. It's about being happy with ourselves when we're all alone or with close friends or in a group of unknowing people. Another way to look at it is... it's loving and enjoying ourselves without expecting everyone to like or love us. Live as an EXAMPLE so that others may follow!

Loving ourselves does not make us any better than anyone else. We're all the same in GOD'S eyes. It's simply about raising the standard to what we will allow into our Belief-System. Letting other people know we do not stoop to the level of self-destruction any longer. Instead, we now respect and love who we are as a Child of GOD, and as a Lady of Purpose!

Could it be we need to set a higher standard for ourselves to enjoy happiness, and live as an example before others that could bring happiness into their lives? YES! That would be an awesome and rewarding goal for each of us TO LIVE BY!

WHAT DO WE MEAN WHEN WE SAY SELF-LOVE?

Many people mistakenly believe that Self-Love is the same as narcissism or having a big ego. It's NOT! So, what do we mean when we say Self-Love? "Self-love means having a high regard for your own well-being and happiness. Self-love means taking care of your own needs and not sacrificing your well-being to please others. Self-love means not settling for less than you deserve" (Brandt, 2018).

You can also add in, *'who may not deserve your time'. (CJ's words)*

We will take Dr. Brandt's statements and go a little deeper... Self-Love means having a high regard for your own wellbeing and happiness...(Dr. Brandt)

- When you don't LOVE your own wellbeing, who else will? Yes, your husband, close friends and family can be there to love you and be by your side through your Journey-Walk, but are they actually in charge of your Brain & Heart? No, they are not, because they do not live in your body. They are not responsible for your beliefs that are stored in your Brain or Heart. YOU are responsible for what you bring into them and believe, and what you allow to stay as Belief-Thoughts. YOU have to answer to GOD for your own beliefs, other human beings cannot do that for you.

Self-Love means taking care of your own needs and not sacrificing your 'own wellbeing' to please others. (Dr. Brandt)

- WOW! Is that one hard pill to swallow? I don't know how many of you Ladies have had to make that sacrifice. Or, you're living at the moment with people in your life that YOU are having to sacrifice your very own wellbeing to please them. May be someone who is very dominating, cold-hearted, plus demand you to think and believe as they do. They are taking over your

144

life in a high energy level of controlling YOU. If you see yourself in a life-style as what I've just described, ask yourself this question... "Do I see Self-Love in my own being?" My guess, you'd answer... "NO."

Ladies, so if Self-Love means... taking care of our own needs and not sacrificing our own wellbeing to please others... does that mean we're shallow, egotistical, selfish to others or self-centered? NO! It means, here again... we have to answer for our own beliefs before GOD, and HE IS NOT going to be happy that we have allowed someone to take away our joy, peace, and present life to someone who doesn't deserve our love and admiration?

GOD tells us in **1 Corinthians 13:13 .... "And now abide in faith, hope, love, these three, but the greatest is LOVE."**

Self-Love means not settling for less than you deserve. (Dr. Brandt)

- As a CHRIST believer, loving ourselves means we should protect ourselves to a higher-belief-point from the negative stuff people throw our way personally. We are much more important than some want us to believe we are. Why do or WHY would we settle for less? Most people have a vague or no idea at all of what Self-Love truly means in GOD'S eyes. Most people will tell you it's a self-serving, narcissistic attitude towards living life. I would agree, to a degree. Yes, some will take it to a level of having the narcissistic attitude part of being self-serving. Don't leave me now, let me explain...

I know when you read or hear about self-severing you think of... just that... serving yourself. Well, Self- Serving can also have a POSITIVE belief-outlook! You have to have a 'belief in your-SELF' that YOU can accomplish what YOU believe in. YOURSELF with all that GOD has for YOU to have, to enjoy, and to become that person you so desire to be!

Ladies, 'If we don't step-up and try – we'll never have!
- A CJism

∽∾

WE are the one who ultimately influences ourselves more than anyone or anything can. That statement right there should tell you how important you are and how to treat yourself.

THERE'S A DIFFERENCE BETWEEN LOVE FOR SELF AND SELF-LOVE.

Keep reading. Someone may say that Self-Love is treating yourself to special things, like going shopping and buying things that maybe you don't necessarily need at the moment or you can't really afford. Or, you treat yourself to a Spa Day, maybe even book a special travel trip you've seen advertised online. All the above may be great, and can be considered an action of LOVE, with the exception of buying things or doing things you can't really afford, because of the strain it may put on your finances.

Shopping, going to the spa or taking a trip are all well and good, and I love doing it. But, when you return and throw all the sacks of purchased items on the sofa, or realize you chipped a freshly manicured fingernail, or upon returning from your nice vacation you discover you're minus one less suitcase, where's your Self-Love then? Do you get it?

Self-Love isn't all about showering ourselves with material things, manicuring our bodies, cruising the waters or hiking the mountain trails. Self-Love is just what it says... LOVE YOURSELF – no matter what happens, whatever people say and even when things goes wrong in your life!

Self-Love is a one-on-one personal relationship with our MIND, HEART and ACTIONS! – A CJism

BE YOUR OWN 'COACH'

Self-Love is another way of saying, Self-COMPASSION, a way of relating to yourself by not harshly judging yourself for every little mistake you make, as well as every time someone speaks negative words into your life or has success in their lives that you so desire to experience. Self-Compassion involves treating yourself with kindness, concern, and support you'd show a family member or friend. When faced with a difficulty in your Journey-Walk, respond to yourself with kindness, rather than harsh Self- Judgement and recognize that imperfection is part of our experience throughout life. Self-Compassion can lighten the load on your shoulders, minds and hearts.

ABOVE ALL... ALLOW GOD TO BE YOUR 'LIFE COACH'

- DON'T dwell in 'the negative-pit' any longer – give it all to JESUS to turn your life around!
- GO TO GOD before you begin harshly belittling yourself – because HE is the ONE who can inwardly give you a Lift in Life!
- LISTEN to HIS guidance and FOLLOW HIM – NEVER LISTEN to the negative people again!
- BE THANKFUL for having a GOD who will NEVER leave you – Nor will HE ever bring up your past once you're forgiven!

Ladies, we have the permission to LOVE ourselves, but not in a self-centered way that leads us to thinking and believing

...'it's all about me.' But, in a Godly way, which leads others to believe GOD can do great wonders in their lives, too.

If we lived in a world that was perfect 24/7, where nothing ever went wrong, where would our sanity be? Think about that. What we must understand is the astonishing fact that we're GOD's artwork. HE must have really loved Eve in the Bible when HE created her. HE loved her after she allowed sin to come into her life. So, HE doesn't feel any differently about you and me. HE created us as well and HE will continue to love us no matter what we look like or how many mistakes we make.

Do yourself an enormous favor... LOVE YOURSELF!! Because, you are GOD's beautiful creation. Don't make HIM sad by being sad and down on yourself. If we're supposed to love our neighbors as ourselves, shouldn't we be fair to ourselves and love ourselves? Another thought on that is... If we are to love our neighbors as ourselves... right now, what level of love would you be giving to your neighbors?

Something to think about, isn't it?

You can LOVE yourself to the point that great things
will come from that LOVE...
Or, you can hate yourself to the point nothing
positive will come into your life!

149

LET'S CARRY THIS THOUGHT WITH US...

Ladies, I have given a fair amount of truths for you to ask this question of yourself... "Can I rise to a high level of Self- LOVE for myself?" Will you? I have given you several definitions and examples to Self-Love. But what I'm about to give you is our heavenly FATHER'S Words of TRUTHS that you should read, remember, and go back often and reread these Scriptures to be reminded. Count how many times you read the word LOVE and feel the message of LOVE.

1 Chronicles 16:34 & Jeremiah 33:11b... "Give thanks to the LORD, for HE is good; HIS LOVE ENDURES FOREVER."

Song of Songs 2:4... "He has taken me to the banquet table and HIS banner over me is LOVE."

Zephaniah 3:17... "The LORD your GOD is with you, the MIGHTY WARR IOR who saves. HE will take great delight in you, in HIS LOVE HE does not rebukes you, HE will rejoice over you with singing."

Romans 8:35-39... More Than Conquerors; "Who shall separate us from the LOVE of CHRIST?"

John 3:16... "For GOD so LOVED the world that HE gave HIS one and only SON, that whoever believes in HIM shall not perish but have eternal life."

1 John 5:20... "We know also that the SON of GOD has come and has given us understanding, so that we may know HIM who is true. And we are in HIM who is true... even in HIS SON JESUS CHRIST. HE is the true GOD and eternal life."

Romans 5:8... But GOD demonstrates HIS own LOVE for us in this... While we were still Sinners, CHRIST died for us.

1 Corinthians 13:13... "Three things will last forever, FAITH, HOPE, and LOVE, and the greatest of these is LOVE.

NOTE TAKING SPACE

Chapter Ten

PRINCIPLE #4 – **SELF–ESTEEM**

According to different dictionaries, Self-Esteem is... "a confidence and satisfaction in oneself" (Self-Esteem, 2020a), "a realistic respect for or favorable impression of oneself" (Self-Esteem, 2020b) and "Self-Esteem, is an individual's subjective evaluation of their own worth (Self-Esteem, 2020c).

According to CJ, Self-Esteem is...The results from taking ACTION, to bringing the lows in Life and Raising them to Higher Levels in Our Self-Worth!

Self-Esteem... We all think we know what that means. Right? Self-Esteem is usually bunched in with Self-Worth, Self-MOTIVATION and maybe one or two of the other Seven Principles of SELF. Let's look at it this way. Having...

- HIGH LEVEL of Self-Esteem plays an important part in our success throughout life.
- TOO LITTLE of Self-Esteem can leave us feeling defeated and depressed or believing... 'Oh well, that's just who I am, I just can't succeed!'
- LOW Self-Esteem can bring on bad choices and we never live up to our full potential.

What we allow to enter into our Belief-System (Brain & Heart) could have an effect on our Self-Esteem and can even destroy it to a degree we then believe we could never build it up or rebuild it back again. But, Ladies, you can! It may take a lot of work on your part to let go of all the Negatives, but it can be accomplished.

How, you ask?

- Having Faith in yourself with giving 'enthusiasm and eagerness' into your own beliefs.
- To regard yourself Positively on the fact you know you can do 'it', whatever 'it' is.
- By seeing yourself with respect and admiration of what you believe you can accomplish!

I've used this verse before, but sometimes we have to be reminded again and again... **"I can do ALL things through CHRIST who strengthens me." Philippians 4:13**

This is true...However, we must do 'our part' too! Having a Positive Self-Esteem is a BLESSING to living a fulfilling life with ourselves and with others. TRUE or FALSE? I hope you said, TRUE.

GOD GIVES US PERMISSION TO BE HAPPY LADIES!

- Our Self-Esteem reflects our judgment to know the degree of our ability to deal with the everyday tasks and trails of our life.
- Self-Esteem reflects on our happiness, successes, at the present and in our future. It also builds the belief within us that we can accomplish our GOALS.

If we're not happy in our LIFE-JOURNEY, we should ask ourselves, why? We may be carrying a load of unnecessary garbage in our Minds and Hearts that we have no need to be carrying around with us? Look at the bold subject title above... there are three prime words in that statement? What are they? The first one is 'GOD' but what's the second and third one? 'HAPPY' and 'LADIES'! 'GOD' GIVES US PERMISSION TO BE HAPPY LADIES'!!!

Ladies, we're not on this earth for very long. Yes, it may seem like an eternity if you live to be 90 or more, but think about this... Life is short, so why do we put ourselves into dark valleys of negative thinking and believing, when we could be soaring high with happiness and truly enjoying life? Good question, isn't it? Answer it for yourself's own understanding where you are in life at this very moment.

The Five Ingredients of SELF-ESTEEM.

Answer HAPPY or NOT HAPPY or AT TIMES, to the statements below...

1. Do I have HAPPINESS within myself in... My understanding of Self-Worth?
2. Do I have HAPPINESS within myself in... My COMPLETENESS as a Lady?
3. Do I have HAPPINESS within myself in... The Self-SATISFACTION of how I'm doing Life?
4. Do I have HAPPINESS within myself in... My I~N~N~E~R PEACE – in my HEART?
5. Do I have HAPPINESS within myself in... COMFORT of who I am as a person?

Were your answers appealing to you? Were they the answers you enjoy seeing? Which one(s) do you see that could need a little more improvement? Let's see what we can do about boosting up those levels. Look at the LEVELS below and 'draw' a box around the number of the one you see yourself in at the moment, and then 'circle' the number of the one you'd love to become more like.

THE FOUR LEVELS of SELF-ESTEEM...

1. Low Self-Esteem – Very little to none
2. False Self-Esteem – I fake a lot of my Self-Esteem for others to see.
3. Comes and Go's Self-Esteem – Often have many different levels of Self-Esteem
4. Higher Plane (Soaring) with Self-Esteem – I hold myself on a high healthy level of Esteem..

Let's start with #4... **High Plane Soaring of Self-Esteem.** Having a Soaring and Positive Self-Esteem is living a fulfilled life within yourself, with others, and LIFE in general. The higher and deeper your self-Esteem is, the better equipped you are to cope with life's adversities. Most likely, you are creative in your work, which means... the more successful you are expected to be in whatever we are pursuing. People who are successful are simply people who have picked themselves up one time more than they were knocked down. They keep their ESTEEM to the highest level of being POSITIVE.

#3... Comes and Go's Self-Esteem... Same as our... ups and downs in life. Examples of some of the Actions of what can happen to take away our Self-Esteem:

- Someone's negative words or statements.
- Someone we care about showing little or no interest in the reason for our high Self-Esteem.
- Something we felt would be Positive turns out bad.
- Can't let go of past failures.
- Our mood at the moment.
- When we're more of a follower than a leader.

Examples of Actions to give us HIGH Self-Esteem:

- The feeling that we have accomplished something we have set out to make happen!
- Our hard work has been rewarded for a job well done.
- We have believed in ourselves that we could do it and we did!

#2. False Self-Esteem ... FAKE Self-Esteem. What and how we betray ourselves before others. We want people to think we are a Positive and well-organized person who knows what we want and we pretend to go after it. When in fact, we may be quite the opposite when alone with our thoughts and no Actions. It's the 'Portray-Mode' we present in front of others that we want people to see, when deep down we cannot see us as beautiful or successful nor 'Someone of Importance.'

#1. Low to No Self-Esteem... Well, I think we all know what this means. It's the lack of Confidence in one's self. When experiencing low Self-Esteem, the elevation of qualities can be very low, and experiencing a good LIFE is on a low grade of belief. Sometimes we experience more emotional stress and shame than what we could ever imagine possible. Low to No Self-Esteem brings in more trouble than we expected. So, why do we go that low, Ladies?

EVEN IF WE FAIL AT ONE OR MORE ATTEMPTS TOWARD SUCCESS, THAT'S BETTER THAN NEVER TRYING AT ALL AND LIVING A LIFE Of REGRET!

ARE YOURS SMALL OR LARGE LABELS?

Here are some of the Labels we pin within ourselves when we have LOW Self-Esteem...Which ones are you familiar with? I feel:

- Not Worthy
- Foolish
- Uncertainty
- Doubt

- Depression
- Inappropriate
- Guilt
- Fear
- Inadequacy
- Insecurity
- Wronged
- Rejected
- Failure
- Not measuring up
- Maybe just tired of trying
- Don't Care anymore!

Unfortunately, any or all the above emotional beliefs could be leading you into... Self-Pity and Misery! Can we not control each of these? Can we not change each of these Labels?

YES, we can! GOD created each of us with our own BRAIN and our own HEART to think on our own and the ability to make our own decisions and choices. So, Ladies, let's take ownership in our SELF and change all the Negatives to POSITIVES for the use of our own wellbeing! Take ownership in our own existence! GOD has plans for you and me, and what HE has given us, HE never intended for us to give that ownership up to anyone or for anything negative!

Albert Einstein once said, "The significant problems we face cannot be solved by the same level of (baggage) thinking that created them (in the first place)!" (Additional words added by CJ)

Which ones are you already enjoying the results from?

- My Abilities
- My Dreams and Goals
- All the POSITIVES in my Life
- Living a Happy and Positive example before others
- My JOY & HAPPINESS
- Living out my Calling from GOD
- Knowing I am WORTHY of my own LOVE and RESPECT

Do you see any that you may need to work on achieving? I'm hoping you are seeing more clearly now and understanding that Self-Esteem is a feeling that feeds off of our RESPONSES, and our ACTIONS!!

Ladies, feed yourself with POSITIVE 'food for thought' and stop listening to those NEGATIVE voices inside you, and the voices that enter through your ears or read with your eyes! With GOD's help, HIS powers and HIS strengths, you can turn yourself around to become that POSITIVE – high Self-

Esteem person you have always had the desire to become. I'm an example of one who stop listening to negative narratives!

It tells us in **Proverbs 4:7a to "Get wisdom"** So, Ladies, you have a Book called the BIBLE and you have Christian Pastors and class teachers, and Christian leaders in every town across our nation, and hopefully Christian friends and family members, who can give you Wisdom on the ways of CHRIST. It's then up to you to take it to Heart and follow GOD'S guidance.

We have to come out of the old-suffocating-suitcase to take ourselves to a much higher level of POSITIVE thinking in order to solve our problems. Once we're out of the old-smelly suitcase, we can see changes happening. We have to make an EFFORT! What level do you desire your Self-Esteem to be? Give yourself a break and soar through life with #4...High Plane Soaring of Self-Esteem! And, see where your attitude and Self-Esteem, Motivation, Confidence and Self- Worth turns out to be! Because Self-Esteem means... The DEGREE to which you ASSIGN WORTH to YOURSELF. Ladies, GOD created us with our own brains to think on our own, just like giving us the ability to breathe on our own. We should be taking ownership in that and put it to use for our own Self. Take ownership in our own existence! GOD has plans for each of us and what HE has given us, HE never intended for us to give that ownership up to anyone else.

Learning how to respond to hardships, adversities and even hitting rock bottom is entirely up to us. We are the creator of our own responses, our thoughts and our actions and reactions.

LET'S CARRY THIS THOUGHT WITH US...

We choose our response on changing the way we see ourselves. All six of the PRINCIPLES of SELF is an expressive feeling that feeds off of our thoughts and responses, and then our Actions! Let's feed ourselves with POSITIVE factual material and thoughts, and STOP listening to those Negative voices inside of us and the Negative voices that are in our faces at times! With GOD's help, HIS Powers and HIS Strength, we can turn ourselves around to become that POSITIVE person we've seen in other people, which we've always wanted to be like but never knew how – well, now we do! Ladies, the person YOU have always dreamed and desired to be... YOU CAN BE!!

Our Self-Esteem reflects and enhances our judgement on our ability to cope with every-day challenges. It also reflects on the blessings that GOD gives that should make us extremely happy. After all, GOD gives us permission to HAPPY! Our Self-Esteem reflects upon our successes in life.

GO NOW OUT INTO THE WORLD AND BE THAT PERSON, and don't forget to take GOD with you every step of the way!

Chapter Ten Reflections

Self-ESTEEM is the results from taking 'ACTION' to bringing the Lows in Life and Raising Them to Higher Levels into Our Self-Worth! We have to take ourselves to a much higher level of thinking in order to solve the problems. We have to come out of the suitcase, before we can see changes happening. We have to make an EFFORT! How we RESPOND to hardships, adversatives or hitting rock bottom is entirely up to us. We are the creator of our own responses.

We should be focusing on OUR Abilities, Dreams and Goals, All the Positives in our Life, Living a Happy and Positive example before others, and Living out our Calling from GOD

Choose our responses – chooses our results! - A CJism

Would you classify your personal JOURNEY-WALK a HAPPY journey? Tell the top three reasons why.

What were the Five Ingredients of Self-Esteem?

Which of THE FOUR LEVELS of Self-Esteem do you place yourself in?

Be truthful with yourself and think about the true statement(s) that fits your life at the moment....~ Not Worthy ~ Foolish ~

Uncertainty ~ Doubt ~ Depression ~ Inappropriate ~ Guilt ~ Fear ~ Inadequacy ~ Insecurity ~ Wronged ~ Rejected ~ Failure ~ Not measuring up ~ Maybe just Tired ~ Don't Care anymore!

Great Wisdom from Charles Swindoll: "The remarkable thing is we have a choice every day regarding the attitude we will embrace for that day. We cannot change our past...we cannot change the fact that people will act in a certain way. We cannot change the inevitable. The only thing we can do is play on the one string we have, and that is our attitude...I am convinced that life is 10% what happens to me and 90% how I react to it. And so it is with you...we are in charge of our attitudes." (Swindoll, 2003)

NOTE TAKING SPACE

Chapter Eleven

PRINCIPLE #5 – **SELF-MOTIVATION**

Our Self-Motivation 'Activates' When We Put Actual Movement into Our Intentions! According to sources, MOTIVATION means, "a physical movement (Motivation, 2020a) or "the general desire or willingness of someone to do something" Motivation, 2020b).

CJ's definition of Self-Motivation is… Having a dream/vision that we so desire to see carried out, and we are MOTIVATED to make a MOVEMENT of ACTION towards experiencing that VISION becoming an ACCOMPLISHMENT.

YOUR VISION

Think of a Project, a Dream, a Physical Goal that you have been thinking about doing. Maybe it's just been presented to you or its been on your mind for a while or maybe for years. You have always envisioned yourself doing it someday or finishing what you have already started working on but found yourself sidetracked for one reason or another. But, this 'vision' is still there in your mind and Heart. Truthfully answer the questions below...

- What is keeping me from my VISION?
- What would it take to MOTIVATE me to 'get up' and begin the process to making it happen?
  - o If your answer was MONEY, then begin right now putting into place A PLAN to soon have that problem solved! Sitting there and doing nothing will get you nowhere fast!
- What benefits/rewards would I be blessed with if I made this VISION into a reality?

Ladies, it always begins with a VISION, and then make it happen! It may be as simple as 'seeing' that the ceiling fan in the living room is adjusted. OR, to the 'VISION' of finishing two more years of college, in order to get your PhD, that has been your DREAM for many years!

Self-Motivation is... movement in your actions! In other words, ... You can't remain seated or stay home with your covers pulled up over your head and do nothing! You have to make a movement in order to see and have action. Can you make things happen when you never move from your tracks? NO! Everyone knows that.

MOVERS MAKE THINGS HAPPEN!

MOTIVATION brings on Movement and Action, then Accomplishments, and then the REWARDS comes forth to be proud of and to enjoy!

All it took for my dream to come true in having a book published was lots of prayer and a simple phone call. But, this was after months of writing pages after pages in a manuscript. Within days I was seeing, and hearing about my 'Dream Becoming A Reality', because GOD had it in HIS plans all along. When it's HIS will and timing, nothing will stop HIM. I will always give HIM praise because HE, was already at work in me!

I had spent years praying for this dream to become true. But, if I had never made that phone call to a friend who placed me with a Publishing Company, nothing would have been put in motion. Do you see my point?

- First comes the DREAM,
- Then the COMMITMENT
- Followed by the PREPARATION – placing everything in place, making needed arrangements, etc.
- During or after the Preparation, MOVEMENT toward the finished project must begin!
- In order for your Dream to Become a REALITY, the FINISH-LINE must be an actual GOAL!

Will everything be as normal around you while your eyes are on the FINISH-LINE? Probably not. So many of my normal chores around our house has been done by my sweet, patient and supportive husband or put on hold. He has gotten very familiar with our vacuum cleaner, dishwasher and where kitchen items go in the kitchen cabinets. We've been eating more sandwiches and frozen dinners than usual. And, my husband has done lots of outdoor grilling, in which I love.

I've had to say 'no' to invites from friends, because I had deadlines to meet. Sometimes I had to get up way before daylight or stay up until the wee hours of the night until I reached a finished deadline. I've also suffered extreme hand, back and neck pain, that I had to make extra visits to my Chiropractor to have relief from the pain. My strained eyes have been a distracting facture as well.

But, it was all worth it! Because why? I DID IT! I finished writing this book! It's called... COMMITMENT to my DREAMS and GOALS! And, Ladies, if I can do it, YOU CAN DO IT TOO!

Ladies, what you desire to experience and accomplish in life, with a strong and steady MOTIVATION, can take you over and above anything you could ever imagine! Keeping Motivated will have Positive effects on you emotionally.

A NOTE OF ADVICE – TRUE BUT SAD...

Why do we allow people to lower our motivation? Who gives them the right and the power to enter our I~N~N~E~R space in order to do such things to us? Sorry to say, Ladies, but...WE DO! How? When we let our guard down and take their untruthful words as truth, then our motivation goes up in smoke. But, do we not have the POWER to stop those words of destruction from entering our Belief-System? YES, WE DO! We've already talked of many ways to not allow it to enter into our Belief-System. So... ALWAYS USE THAT POWER, LADIES!

Our question for today should be... If others try and possess such power over us, then why can't WE have even more powers to NOT ALLOW their words or Actions to have an effect on us? Why don't we use such powers that GOD has provided for us to use? GOD is the ONE who can help us remain strong, when others are trying to weaken us!

This would be the time when we should stay MOTIVATED and put Movement in our REACTIONS and kindly walk away with CLOSED EARS and STAY PRAYED UP for protection!

Psalms 138:8... "The LORD will fulfill HIS purpose for me; YOUR love, O LORD, endures forever, do not abandon the works of YOUR hands."

We are the 'works of GOD'S hands.' HE was our CREATOR in the womb, and HE is also the SUPERIOR throughout our lives as we are HIS Workmanship!

LET'S GET MOTIVATED, LADIES!

Ephesians 3:16... "I pray that out of HIS glorious riches HE may strengthen you with power through HIS SPIRIT in your I~N~N~E~R being".

HOW CAN YOU HELP OTHERS STAY MOTIVATED?

I'll share with you what I experienced while I was finishing the writing of this book. I'm so thankful and blessed by friends and family members who stood beside me during this writing and waiting time. The phone calls, texts and emails were always a blessing to me and my husband, David! We were blessed by friends bringing over meals while I had my head in and hands on this computer. Hearing and reading encouraging words from each one who took the time to send them my way, helped keep me motivated more than they will ever know!

Ladies, always stay connected with those who are working toward their 'Dream Becoming A Reality'. If you can't join them, let them know often that you are praying for them, because you'll never know how much a few words from time to time gives them motivation to continue on until their mission is completed. Be that 'special friend'!

LET'S CARRY THIS THOUGHT WITH US...

Make a Movement within your Self-Motivation towards rising your Self-Respect, Self-Love, Self-Esteem, Self-Confidence and Self-Worth to much higher levels on the 'ole scale. Our Self-Motivation activates MOVEMENT that brings on ACTIONS = RESULTS!

What results do we see when we are highly motivated? Great and Wonderful Happenings!!

Chapter Eleven Reflections

Self-Motivation is putting Actual Movement Into Our Intentions! Our Self-Motivation activates when we... Make a MOVEMENT with ACTION. MOVERS MAKES THINGS HAPPEN! MOTIVATION brings on Movement, Action and then Accomplishments! Keeping MOTIVATED will have Positive effects on us emotionally, creatively and spiritually.

Ephesians 3:16... "LORD, I pray that out of YOUR glorious riches YOU will strengthen me with power through YOUR SPIRIT in my INNER being."

When are you the most motivated?

When are you the least motivated?

What has happened in the past that has destroyed your motivation? NOW, LET IT GO!!!

What are some of the things people have said that has brought down your motivation? NOW, LET IT GO!!!

WHAT is SIGNIFICANT in your life at this moment?

What Results DO WE SEE When We Are Highly MOTIVATED? GREAT & WONDERFUL THINGS!

YOUR MEMORY VERSE: HIS divine power has given us everything we need for a godly life... 2 PETER 1:3 (through 8)

NOTE TAKING SPACE

Chapter Twelve

PRINCIPLE #6 – **SELF-CONFIDENCE**

According to sources, Self-Confidence is, "Belief in oneself; determination; certainty; spirit: if you feel confidence, you feel sure about your abilities, qualities or ideas" (Self-Confidence, 2020a), Confidence in oneself and in one's powers and abilities" (Self-Confidence, 2020b).

According to CJ, Self-Confidence is: a Positive belief, causing a Positive state of mind about what and how we can accomplish goals and what we can physically accomplish by setting goals and seeing them through to completion!

What do we do when we're struggling with having the strength and commitment to doing something about reaching our goals? KEEP ON PUSHING FORWARD!! Because the rewards are much more powerful than the regrets!

PART A – SELF-CONFIDENCE

I think we know what it's all about to have or not to have confidence in ourselves. Right? Ask yourself if you have a hard time with your own Self-Confidence. Would my hand go up if I asked that question? Well, since you can't see me in person at the moment, I'll fib a little and say... No, it didn't go up... wwwelllll maybe half way! Okay, yes, my hand went up! You can laugh at me if you'd like, that's one thing we all need in our lives... MORE LAUGHTER! Yes, I still struggle with Self-Confidence at times. Although, nothing like I used to, for sure. From time-to-time, something challenging arises, and I find me telling myself... "You can do this! You can do this. YOU CAN DO THIS, CJ!" At times I blame it on the fact I'm getting older, but then GOD tells me... "I'm not finished with you yet, my child, so get up and get going!"

Let's talk a moment about these five REALIZING POINTS...

The best accomplishment we experience is realizing we can have Self-Confidence within ourselves in the times when:

1. We take into account the mistakes we've made 'in our past': We all have a past, some great – some not so good. Some things in our past we're proud of – some we're not so proud of. But, when we demonstrate Self-

Confidence, people who've known using the past can witness that we have moved on from the mistakes and found a way to up-the-value in our CONFIDENCE!

2. Regardless of our weaknesses we stay strong: We all have our share of weaknesses and strengths within us. But it's what we pull from our past to prepare and improve for the present and future that tells of our Self-Confidence... that we can actually 'do it'!

3. We feel CONFIDENT despite our imperfections: Ladies, I would ask you... Who on this earth is PERFECT? Is there one single person that has walked on this earth, other than our LORD JESUS CHRIST, who has a Perfect Past or Present? NO ONE! We are all from a fault-filled-'human'-race, so my point is simply... NO ONE IS PERFECT! But, we can and should feel we've accomplished something good or great and that we're worthy of receiving at least an 'atta-girl' recognition from time to time. Right? Ladies, I say, be proud of your ACCOMPLISHMENTS! Not to the degree of being overly boastful, arrogant or mean-minded, but walk with CONFIDENCE before and after you have accomplished your goal! Let's say, your dream has come true because you have overcome all the obstacles. I say you now deserve an Authentic Milestone of Accomplishment Award!!!! Hey, I like those last five words, don't you? Meaning,

you are not fake, you have not cheated, nor have you given up. You have accomplished a milestone by having CONFINDENCE in yourself! Ladies, let's feel gratified, despite our imperfections!

4. Self-Confidence in My Gratifications and My Imperfections – which have I learned the most from? Great question! I'm sure your answer was... my gratifications. Right? Well, that's a good answer, however, let's look slightly deeper into our imperfections as lessons. What would your answers be if you answered truthfully:

   o What have my imperfections taught me about what I can accomplish? Anything? Anything at all? Whatever your answer was, is there a 'lesson' within that imperfection that now can be changed into a Positive result?

   o Have I learned yet how to make the changes in my imperfections into having more gratifications to reward myself?

   o Am I willing to make the changes in my imperfections??

5. The best feeling we can have is having Self-Confidence in ourselves... by being courageous enough to stand up for ourselves: That statement explains itself. Ladies, let's STAND UP for ourselves and never again allow anyone to kill our Self-Confidence. They receive

NOTHING from taking it away from us except false and arrogant pride. But, for us, we will lose a lot! Guard your wellbeing and never, I say NEVER allow anyone to take away your Authentic Milestone of Accomplishment Award that you deserve by having CONFIDENCE in yourself!

"BLOSSOM TIME"
HOW DO WE WALK WITH CONFIDENCE?

Has there ever been a time in your life that you can label as... your BLOSSOM TIME? A time that maybe you had just come out of a horrible experience, a very low point in life that you didn't think you could ever crawl out of it? I called them... Journey-Crawls. But then your life began to show some LIGHT. And, then great things started to happen, and you began to BLOSSOM again! You regained your Self-Confidence!

I've been there more than once in my lifetime, many times actually. The one time I'll share with you was when I was still recovering from the marriage and death of my abusive husband. I had returned to runway modeling to try and regain some my Self-Confidence. Because, taking to a runway in front a room filled with total strangers requires a lot of courage, especially when you've been away from it for a few years. I remember thinking while modeling the garments,

'Am I walking properly? Did I make my turn correctly? Did I present the garment with the attitude to show Ladies they need this particular garment?' And, on and on the insecurities went that first trip on the runway, after several years being away from modeling. But, I think I pulled it off pretty well, because I was asked to do more shows on later dates.

This was in 1988, when I was so fortunate to have met and modeled on the runway with Miss USA. This was a big event in my hometown, since it was a televised fashion show, sponsored by JCPenney's. Now, Ladies, if something to that level of excitement couldn't have lifted my confidence, I don't know what would have. Miss USA's dressing room was right beside mine and we both came out into the open space at the same time and began talking. She was very young and beautiful. I'll never forget, she was so nervous because she'd just received her title of MISS USA 1988 only a short time prior to this style show. I think this must have been her first style show after receiving her crown. And, being several years older, I found myself speaking words of calmness and encouragement to her. Who would have ever believed that?

Isn't it awesome when GOD places us in the right place at the right time when we or someone else needs to be uplifted for whatever reason? My spirits were uplifted, believe me, because I was now talking to our beautiful Miss USA and she seemed to become less nervous while we visited. She only had one other person traveling with her to this event and the lady was busy organizing the apparel items in the dressing room.

I remember, I went out on the stage with the other Ladies first to do our runway walk and presentation of the garments we were wearing, then went back to our dressing rooms to change for the next show of garments. She was still standing there, and she complemented me on my performance... again, I was uplifted! We modeled a few more garments, and then I changed and went back to the stage for the last walk. We were to outline the stage and look back at the entrance for the last grand entry of Miss USA. I was about halfway in the middle of the lineup on the right side. The beautiful Miss USA made her walk both ways on the stage and stopped in the center at the front, she did her hand wave a few more times as the packed crowd cheered. She then turned around and walked back to the entry doors and as she walked by, she looked right at me and mouthed words that looked like she was saying, "Thank you". She then walked off the stage. She was thanking me for being a comforting person to her, go figure that!

All the models walked around the stage. We did our wave and exited the runway and went back to our dressing rooms. I didn't see her again until we stood before her to get a personal autographed picture. She raised up from her chair and actually gave me a quick hug and I introduced her to my sons. We had a very short visit, as there were what seemed like a hundred people waiting in line to meet her.

Ladies, please understand, you don't have to have experiences like what I just told you in order to experience BLOSSOM TIMES. It could be any of the times when you felt like you were a winner instead of a loser. Such as when you overcome your fears and rely on your Self-Confidence to carry you through. It could be a time when you achieved an honor at work or in an organization you are in currently. And, what about the times you hear your child say they love you or your husband tells you he is so proud of you? It could also be your wedding, a promotion at work or just as simple as someone saying something nice to you that was unexpected. I could continue on and on, but I know you see the point I'm making.

BLOSSOM TIMES are blessings to our being. In this day and age, we need all we can get. These things make us feel complete, loved, appreciated and, maybe, even honored. What about giving others their BLOSSOM TIMES? What A BLESSING to be A BLESSING!

Each day, we need to ask GOD to place someone in our path that we can be a blessing to as well. It could begin a BLOSSOM TIME for them. You'll never know what they can or will do with an encouragement to help them reach a goal, or a dream they've had on their TO DO list that helps them experience a BLOSSOM TIME. TRY IT, AND SEE!

"Cultivate I~N~N~E~R beauty, the gentle, gracious kind that GOD delights in…" 1 Peter 3:4 (MSG)

Our own Personal CONFIDENCE begins from within our SELF, because we are the 'carrier' of our own SELF CONFIDENCE – so carry it graciously so others can see and live by your example! – A CJism

PART B –INNER BEAUTY versus OUTWARD BEAUTY

We can always put on a 'show' and pretend we are someone we really are not. We can put on an arrogant façade that, sooner or later, could turn people away from us. We can even use adjustment charm before others, but we fool no one! (Adjustment charm is when we are Positive one moment, but then adjust our charm to arrogancy.) In order to walk in the path of GOD'S Gracefulness, we must be true to ourselves and let our true grace shine through.

'Charm is deceptive, and beauty is fleeting; but a woman who fears (respects, honors and worships) the LORD is to be praised.' Proverbs 31:30 (NIV)

In this day and time, it's hard to believe beauty is more than skin deep. Right? In my opinion that's a 'skin deep expression!' Beauty is much more than just what we see with our eyes, in the mirror, on the surface.

You know what, Ladies? There's nothing wrong with our 'natural' outward beauty! Whhhat? Did I just say that? Yes, I did, because, that's how GOD created us! But, if we want some improvement on our outward appearance to enhance our beauty, that's soooo okay.

As I've mentioned before, there's all types of actions we can take to improve how we look in front of others. We have tons of books, videos, online classes, etc. etc., on how to improve our outward beauty. So, with all the cosmetics we have available to us and classes on how to apply them, we can create attractive improvements on our outward beauty!

The outward presentation of our appearance of beauty... in other words, our highlighted faces, our hairstyles, the copycatting of new fashion designs that complement our bodies – we do it all to make us what? To feel better about ourselves? To look pretty? Correct?

So, where does our REAL natural beauty truly come from anyway? It's from within our MINDS, our HEARTS, our

VOICES, and our ACTIONS..., our ACTIONS toward ourselves, other people and happenings!

Yes, our outward beauty can be tucked, scraped, sculpted by paint, and dressed up pretty. But, when the inside foundation is weak, we're in trouble! Because, all the paint in this nation will not hold a freckle to the beauty we keep captive inside us. The outward presentation of our appearance of beauty, in other words... our painted faces, our hairdos, and the clothes we wear, will eventually be washed off or faded away, smeared below our eyes, while our hair will be combed out, and our clothes thrown in the dirty clothes hamper. Now, how's that as a visual picture, is that beauty?

See the picture here? Ladies, our beauty is much more than our outward appearance. The outward presentation of our beauty will always need constant repairs, trying new do's, and creating fashion copycats.

I ask you Ladies, is this where you want to place all your 'definition' of beauty? Is this where you want to place all your 'identity' of beauty, with something that will be washed off, faded away, smeared, combed out, and end up in the dirty clothes hamper? Because, if this is where your identity of beauty lies, you're missing out on what GOD'S had planned for you before you were brought into living-being.

Okay, I'm not saying we can't tuck, scrape, and sculpture our faces with paint to look even more beautiful. I'm not saying we shouldn't wear clothes that complement our bodies to help make us feel better about ourselves. What I'm saying is that all these things eventually come off and then we have the bare facts of who we really are right in front of us. I'm not only talking about our stripped physique, but what's inside our HEARTS, and MINDS and our CHARACTER. Those things are with us 24/7.

It's not only the outward appearance of beauty that makes up the person other people see. It's mainly what's inside of you that shines through for others to see and follow as an example, that truly makes you A BEAUTIFUL PERSON!

TO WRAP IT UP... I can teach you how to walk, stand, and carry yourself and, yes, even sit properly, along with how to move your hands, head and feet while walking. I can professionally paint your face and dress you up, and make heads turn by doing an extreme makeover on your outward appearance, without you ever going under the knife. I can show you how to capture people's attention, while you're walking on the runway or simply entering a room! I can show you how to shine with your outward beauty by using your eyes and your smile. And get this... I can show you how to gracefully walk up and down staircases.

189

I can show, within seconds, how to look like you've taken off pounds by the way you stand and carry yourself, while wearing the right clothes. I can do all of that for you. But, Ladies, you will never truly feel beautiful about yourself until you repair or learn what your I~N~N~E~R BEAUTY is all about! Once you come off that runway or leave a room, you'll return back to the person you used to be unless you know your personal I~N~N~E~R BEAUTY. All a runway is, is a show. This is a choice you have to make, whether or not you want to remain the same or live a bless-filled life of knowing and living your I~N~N~E~R BEAUTY. How much "SHOW" will you put on to pretend before others? Wouldn't you want to be a fully Self-CONFIDENT LADY instead, and drop all the pretending?

That was me. I knew everything to do to show off the garment I was wearing on that runway. But, when I packed up my bag to return to the real world, I was back to being the real me. The me who was always down on myself. The me who had no Self-Esteem, and no Self-Worth. The me who never could believe in herself as an individual one-person-being! I felt I always had to be what others wanted me to be. I believed I had to have the approval of the people in my life, before I could ever think of me as a whole person.

I was the person that everyone had said wouldn't ever amount to anything, that I was a loser, and a failure at everything. And, the sad thing about it, Ladies, that was my belief for many years! I was the perfect example of an abused grown woman, by a grown man who said he loved me, but leaving me with no Self-Worth or Self-Respect, nor any Self-Esteem. I allowed him to take it all!

Praise GOD, I am NO LONGER THAT PERSON! And, great things began to happen in my life! And, Ladies, if you battle with no Self-Confidence as well, you need to find the willingness inside of you to change and stay POSITIVE, with a new and great Self-Confidence within yourself!

LET'S CARRY THIS THOUGHT WITH US...

You've read a lot about my life story in this book. All the turmoil, the dark valleys and losses I've endured. And soon you'll read about the time I tried to take my own life. But, just look at me now, my Self-IMPORTANCE is at the highest level it has ever been in my entire life, and for many reasons! For one reason, having a dream for many years to publish a book, and IT'S HAPPENED!!! I will finish my second BOOK soon! It's meant for you Single Ladies!

DREAMS do come TRUE; PRAYERS will be ANSWERED in GOD's TIMING and in HIS way. You will see how your life can change, because you started believing in yourself! Ladies, NEVER GIVE UP! Keep working toward your GOALS and BELIEVE IN YOURSELF! Keep a STRONG and SOLID STAND 'IN' your Self- CONFIDENCE, and never, no never, stop relying on GOD!!!

Ladies, when you walk into a room, make heads turn! Remind those around you that, not only do you walk in CONFIDENCE, but you have the KEY, yes, the KEY, to something they want... your RELIANCE TO LIFE! What do I mean by 'reliance'? It's your reliance upon GOD that gives you this healthy Self-Worth. Also, it's your CONFIDENCE that you can accomplish great things and overcome all past and present roadblocks! You can show others how they, too, can have the power of GOD'S Spirit within them to help them through their life, every second of the day and night.

GOD has given you the strength, and the CONFIDENCE to become the BEAUTIFUL LADY that HE'S had planned for you all along! LADIES, go out into the world and show that you have the CONFIDENCE WALK and POSTURE IN YOURSELF, BECAUSE OF CHRIST JESUS!!!

Take this verse to Heart... **"The LORD appeared to us saying, "I have loved you to myself with an everlasting love; I will build you up again, and you will be rebuilt. Again, you will** take up your tambourines and go out to dance with the joyful." Jeremiah 31:3-4

Chapter Twelve Reflections

Self-Confidence is a Positive belief, causing a Positive state of mind about what and how we can accomplish our goals. You are not fake, you have not cheated nor have you not given up. Ladies, let's feel gratified despite our imperfections! Our own Personal CONFIDENCE begins from within our-SELF, because we are the 'carrier' of our own SELF CONFIDENCE – so carry it graciously so others can see and live by your example! DREAMS do come TRUE; PRAYERS will be ANSWERED in GOD'S TIMING, and we can see how our LIVES can CHANGE, because we first BELIEVED IN OURSELVES. So, Ladies, NEVER GIVE UP! Keep working toward your GOALS and BELIEVE IN YOURSELF. Keep a STRONG and SOLID STAND 'IN' your Self-Confidence, and never stop relying on GOD!

LADIES, go out into the world and show that you have the CONFIDENCE WALK and POSTURE IN YOURSELF, BECAUSE OF CHRIST JESUS!

What does this statement mean? 'found a way to up the 'value' in our CONFIDENCE!'

We've all had 'BLOSSOM TIMES.' What is one that changed your life?

Is my outward appearance where I want to place all my identity, to be known only as my definition of beauty?

Where does our REAL natural beauty truly come from anyway?

Is there anything wrong with dressing up our outward appearance to make us feel beautiful?

WHY?

"Be careful, then, how you live... not as unwise but as wise." Ephesians 5:15

NOTE TAKING SPACE

Chapter Thirteen

PRINCIPLE #7 – **SELF–WORTH**

According to the dictionary, Self-Worth is, "A feeling that you are a good person, who deserves to be treated with respect" (Self-Worth, 2020a), "The sense of one's own value or worth as a person" Self-Worth, 2020b).

Self-Worth, according to CJ, is, personally, related to our Self-Respecting Actions that also can be described as the motive to prevent failure into our lives. For when our Self-WORTH is strong, we can and will accomplish more towards our dreams and goals.

WHAT DO OTHERS CONTRIBUTE TO OUR SELF-WORTH?

First off, let's get this thought out of the way… not allowing others to bring us down can be a frequent inconvenience but may need to be done. Putting walls-of-protection up around our Self-Worth may be the only assurance we have, in order to know we can have the CONFIDENCE to accomplish our GOALS. So, don't be afraid to protect yourself!

Ladies, we need to realize what it is that GOD has placed within us, because, remember, GOD MAKES NO MISTAKES and HE MADE NO junk when creating us! Unfortunately, we are the ones who create the JUNK in our lives or allow it to enter into our Belief-System!

Have you ever noticed that people who have high levels of Self-Confidence and Self-Worth tend to be happier and more content with themselves? They tend to come across as undoubtedly able to handle accomplishments and adversities. Wouldn't you like to be more of a self-assured person? Ladies, you CAN BE!

What should you do if you believe you have low Self-WORTH, and how can you improve in this area? Like I mentioned before ... First, our SELF... RESPECT, LOVE, ESTEEM, MOTIVATION, and CONFIDENCE builds our Self-WORTH! Begin Positively building-up these five PRINCIPLES and keep them built up. And, together they will build your Self-WORTH into a stronger belief in yourself. Also, PRINCIPLE #1 – your Self-Concept – will be raised to a higher POSITIVE percentage level of what and how you think of yourself.

Unfortunately, too many of us go through painful and belittling experiences that makes it difficult for us to have or rebuild a high and healthy Self-Worth. We should always hold healthy boundaries with those who do not uphold us as worthy and are not respectful to our I~N~N~E~R Beliefs.

- Our Self-Worth is what we feel we are worth to ourselves, to others, in our jobs and community, etc. To what degree do we allow others to talk down to us and not fightback? Good question. However, the best answer may be to walk away. If at all possible, walk away from those who tear us down and try to take away our respect, love, esteem, motivation, confidence and soon... our Self-Worth? Ladies, we may need to have and keep STRONGER BOUNDARIES in order to help keep our Self-Worth!

- Our Self-WORTHINESS ... As a child of GOD, as a Lady, a friend, girlfriend, wife, mother or grandmother, employer/employee, teacher, neighbor, etc. – we all deserve to be treated with WORTHINESS, for we are all GOD'S creations! It begins with us doing our part to give RESPECT and LOVE to all those around us. Then, we desire to receive and gain WORTHINESS from others.

As stated in... Dictionary.com – WORTHINESS is '...the 'quality' of deserving attention and respect.' Do we need to work more on our Self-Worth? We all do to some degree, and some more than others. But, Ladies, we have GOD in our corner, to help in all areas of our Self-Worth – WORTHINESS that we're weak in at times!

There's nothing more beautiful than a Lady who carries herself with HONOR, CONFIDENCE and BELIEVING in her Self-Worth! When you do, your Positive personality will radiate from you and you'll find fewer people wanting to take advantage of you. They will see that you are a LADY of Self-Assurance, and Positiveness and a Lady of WORTHINESS!! They will not see you as a 'Mousy – Burger'! NO ma'am! NOT YOU!!! No Mousy – Burger in you!!!

Now, why do I use the word 'Mousy'? Because, what does a mouse do upon seeing a human? They run quickly and hide! We don't do that, right, Ladies? NO, we stand respectfully and show we have Self-Worth and no one will be taking it away from us! Why do I use the word, Burger...? I don't know, it was just the word that has always rolled off of my tongue after saying...Mousy. (LOL) You are allowed to laugh at me again. I love it!

Ladies, we must never forget .... **"We Are Ladies of Promise,
Perseverance and Purpose...
Filled with JOY & HAPPINESS!"**

WHAT WILL YOUR LEGACY BE?

LIFE is a onetime offer, so how well are you using it? We only
have so long on this earth, AND, once we leave this earth, we
cannot have 'DO OVERS'! Duh! Ladies, how are you living
your life at this moment? Is it in a way you would like to have
lived it the first time around? If not, from this point on, your
life can be different! If you're already in a great state of mind
in the '7 PRINCIPLES of SELF,' I say... GREAT JOB!!!
Keep it up!

If you don't have goals, dreams or desires for a more POSITIVE
PRESENT LIFE, what do you have to look forward to in the
FUTURE, while you reside on this earth? There's so much we
all could be doing to experience a higher Self-Worth. And, we
have so much more to accomplish, as well as to give to help
others reach their potential in the 7 PRINCIPLES of LIFE!

So, Ladies... DON'T quit now, DON'T give up now. Today is
the first day of the rest of our lives... MAKE TODAY COUNT
and TOMORROW and ALL THE DAYS THEREAFTER,
until GOD calls you home to be with HIM!

We've talked about how the inward 'work' has to happen before the outward 'walk' can become great. Well... we also have to have CONFIDENCE in ourselves, and feel WORTHY, before the POSITIVE-WALK can begin! So, what about your OUTWARD WALK? What does your WALK in LIFE say about you?

WHAT DO WE LEARN IN THE VALLEYS?

Before reading this next segment, get your Bible out and read the entire Chapter of **Psalms 23**.

The purpose in sharing a few segments of my life with you is to let you know, the valleys in our lives can be where we learn the most, where we can actually begin to repair our lives and begin to grow stronger, to heal. It's the place where we should begin a new and better life and, possibly, a new lifestyle.

After living in Colorado for a few years, the mountains were beautiful, of course, no doubt about that. But I concluded that it's in the valleys where you see so much more amazing beauty. The trickling streams and rushing rivers, the huge beautiful trees and breathtaking flowers, and the fresh mountain air is so cleansing. Also, we see the wildlife much closer, and possibly an American Eagle, which I saw once. So, to me, it always seemed like a 'Healing-VALLEY,' a place to allow all troubles and worries to be cleansed from me. I always felt so cleansed and motivated upon arriving home. There are great places in the Valley to sit and take in the beauty and pray to our CREATOR, our Heavenly GOD!

My point here is… when you find yourself in the 'Healing-VALLEY' after something or someone has pushed you off your feet, or something has knocked the breath out of your life… rejoice that GOD is also in the VALLEY with you! Sometimes, we need a fresh encounter with our SAVIOR to see all there is to see. HIS strength will lift you up, believe me, I know from years of being knocked into a 'deep dark pit' and then I found the 'Healing-VALLEY.' In the meantime, while you're in the 'HEALING-Valley,' look around, look up, look at all the beauty that surrounds you, all the healing that can take place inside of you, then pull yourself up by your high heel shoes, or bootstraps (for the men), and begin your journey up the mountain to accomplish great and mighty things. Learn from the 'pit' and cherish your time in the 'HEALING-Valley.' After asking for healing, maybe ask for forgiveness as well, if it is needed. Pray for the path ahead to be clear and brightly lighted.

Ladies, you must allow GOD to do great wonders in your life. It's up to us whether we'll continue to stay in the dark places or move ourselves to higher ground. When you choose to stay there, this is when you truly need your SAVIOR'S help. Our GOD, who is at the top of the mountain, is the same GOD who will pull you out of the pit and HE can do great wonders in your life!

Spiritually Speaking... Not to take away from the amazing beauty of the mountains, but don't take away the incredible advantages of GOD'S 'HEALING-Valleys'

We serve the GOD WHO planned the Beginning and HE has also planned the end. HE has not left anything in between to chance. HE has planned that as well. GOD has already planned a 'Present-Day-Walk,' while we're upon this earth, and an 'Eternal-Destiny' for us, when we leave this earth.

The BIBLE reveals, and makes it clear, that life is a Gift from GOD, a treasure to be cherished and honored! And, we as Ladies are a unique blend of talents, beauty, and character. And, we are beautiful, and we are SOMEBODY in the eyes of our GOD!

Have you ever known of GOD making a mistake? To be honest with you, I believed HE did with me once in my past, while going through some of the painful paths I experienced. I questioned whether I was created to only endure Heartbreaks, pain, abuse, etc. But, upon looking back now, I have to admit,

"I" chose those paths myself, not GOD! It was NOT the cause of GOD making a mistake in my creation.

No, it was me not relying on GOD to guide me in 'my decision making', not going to HIM in prayer to guide me in my choices. So, no, Ladies, HE didn't make a mistake creating us – most of our turmoil in life is from our own choices! Own up to your mistakes, ask forgiveness and ask for a renewal to begin in your life, and then... Continue to stay in communication with your CREATOR and talk to HIM daily in asking for HIS guidance.

GOD tells us in HIS WORD, how HE LOVES us and how HE thinks of us as HIS creation. But, until we take it to MIND and HEART, we will never walk in the CONFIDENCE WALK or model to others our POSTURE IN CHRIST!

**JOHN 3:30... "HE must become greater:
I must become less."**

READ Psalms 23 again, and I'll... SEE YOU AT THE TOP of the MOUNTAIN!

POSTURE IN CHRIST: "GOD'S GRACEFULLNESS"

When we model ourselves after the image of CHRIST, before others, we are modeling...

- CONFIDENCE THROUGH GOD
- GOD'S POSTURE THROUGH US
- OUR BEAUTY from WITHIN
- GOD'S GRACEFULNESS!
- OUR SOLID BELIEF IN KNOWING WHO WE HAVE IN OUR HEARTS and BY OUR SIDE.

THE 'POINT' IS? Gracefulness is done through our CHARACTER, our ACTIONS. It's about how we TALK before others or to them personally, and how we CARRY ourselves with CONFIDENCE and RESPECT in knowing that we belong to the MIGHTIEST of all kings... KING JESUS!

We no longer have to fear what others may say or think about us.
We no longer have to walk in the shadows of others.
We no longer have to hide behind our past failures!
Because, we are DAUGHTERS of THE KING &
We have a strong Posture in our Walk with HIM! - A CJism

Ladies, let's shout out an AMEN!

All who come before GOD and ask for forgiveness and accept HIM as LORD and SAVIOR into their Hearts are then made a new creation through the blood that was shed on the CROSS for us! It tells us this in John 3:16.

Ladies, we were fashioned by the 'MASTER'S HANDS', HE made us beautiful, but our beauty from within MUST SHINE through! Our beauty is rooted in our I~N~N~E~R Self-Beliefs! Therefore, our beauty must be modeled after GOD'S likeness! This is what our Self-Worth should be built upon. So, Ladies, KEEP YOUR BELIEFS IN YOURSELF STRONG and stay TUNED IN WITH GOD for GUIDANCE!!!

You can now hold your heads high; your Hearts open to share what GOD has done in your life, and let your voice ring out loudly with the true announcement... "I AM A SOMEBODY BECAUSE OF CHRIST JESUS!!!" Let's get EXCITED, LADIES!

To paraphrase a quote, in order for people to treat you well, there must be something deep inside you that sends out a message saying, "I AM A SOMEBODY, BECAUSE GOD MADE ME TO BE A SOMEBODY! I may not be twenty-one and wear a size seven; I may be seventy-one and wear a size twenty-seven, but I AM A SOMEBODY!!!" When you send out a message like that, other people will pick up on it!"

Ladies, we really need those Words of Wisdom in this day and age, and in this time with all the turmoil our world is in today! The world needs strong CHRISTIAN LADIES to stand up and proclaim the POWERS within and through JESUS CHRIST – to UNITE IN CHRIST – NOT SEPARATE!

Be truthful with yourself... Has the quality of BEAUTY in your I~N~N~E~R SELF been hitting rock-bottom lately, or has it been topping the scales with pleasing Self-Worth? Do you now feel like shouting and singing... "I AM BEAUTIFUL BECAUSE I AM A MASTERPIECE OF THE KING ABOVE ALL KINGS!" SING IT, LADIES!!!!

"I am like an olive tree flourishing in the house of GOD; I trust in GOD's unfailing love for ever and ever."
Psalm 52:8 (NIV)

PRINCIPLE #1. which is Self-Concept, is the 'file holder' which holds all the documents that shape our Self-Worth. Within that Self-Concept 'file holder' are the other six PRINCIPLES. They are our...Self-RESPECT, Self-LOVE, Self-ESTEEM, Self-MOTIVATION, Self-COFIDENCE, all of which builds up PRINCIPLE #7... our Self-WORTH! GOD MAKES NO MISTAKES and HE MADE NO JUNK when created us! There's nothing more beautiful than a Lady who carries herself with honor, CONFIDENCE and believing in her Self-Worth!

We Are LADIES of Promise, Perseverance and Purpose!" Inward 'work' has to happen before the outward 'walk' can become great.

GOD tells us in HIS WORD how HE LOVES us and how HE thinks of us as HIS creation. But, until we take it to MIND and HEART, we will never walk in the CONFIDENCE or model to others our POSTURE IN CHRIST!

Ladies, be truthful with yourself – has the quality of BEAUTY in your I~N~N~E~R SELF been hitting rock-bottom lately, or has it been topping the scales with Self-Worth? Do you now feel like shouting and singing... "I AM BEAUTIFUL,

BECAUSE I AM A MASTERPIECE OF THE KING ABOVE ALL KINGS!" SING IT, LADIES!!!!

REMEMBER THIS, LADIES... *"Once we leave this earth, we cannot have 'DO OVERS'!" So, do all you need to do...NOW!!!* A CJisum

What is the #1 thing you have learned while dwelling in a low VALLEY time?

WHAT WILL YOUR LEGACY BE?

REMEMBER THIS LADIES... Once you leave this earth, we cannot have 'DO OVERS'!!! So, do all you need to do... NOW!!

NOTE TAKING SPACE

Chapter Fourteen

HAVING THE CONFIDENCE WALK AND POSTURE IN CHRIST

HAVING the CONFIDENCE WALK... Having the Confidence that we can walk through the bumpy roads, roadblocks and the raging waters that LIFE throws at us. Also, 'walking with confidence and belief in ourselves' that we can reach the top of the mountain of success we are wanting to achieve, small or LARGE!

POSTURE IN CHRIST... Realistically Speaking... Standing Straight Up and Walking with assurance in knowing GOD is beside us all the way! Standing straight up in HIS WORD!

What Does It Mean to Have 'The CONFIDENCE WALK and POSTURE IN CHRIST'?

Let's review the 7 PRINCIPLES ...

- 1st PRINCIPLE – Self-CONCEPT; a picture of what we 'see and believe' in our overall beliefs; our perceptions of what we take into our Belief-System and believe as the truth about ourselves.

- 2nd & 3rd PRINCIPLES – Self-RESPECT & Self-LOVE is totally different, because it's the 'reality of action' in how we respect and love ourselves to the degree of building our Self-Worth. These two Principles are from the beliefs that induces the activity in our MINDS & HEARTS.

- 4th & 5th PRINCIPLES – Self-ESTEEM & Self-MOTIVATION; are 'ACTION MOVEMENTS', meaning, ESTEEM and MOTIVATION only happens when our SECOND & THIRD PRINCIPLES have been put into place. Having ESTEEM & MOTIVATION gets us up and going and becoming productive toward our GOALS.

- 6th PRINCIPLE – Self-CONFIDENCE is 'knowing– having a mental sensational belief that our overall GOALS can be accomplished so that continuing to go forward is meant to be a WINNER! CONFIDENT in BELIEVING in ourselves is a major function within our I~N~N~E~R thoughts and beliefs.

- 7th PRINCIPLE – Self-WORTH is the 'CROWN we receive' upon having a high evaluation within Principles 2–6! Going THROUGH OBSTACLES, NEVER GIVING UP, WORKING HARD, and STAYING POSITIVE will give us the WINNER'S CROWN... Self-Worth!

ALSO, know this... our WORDS, ACTIONS, RESPONSES, ATTITUDE, ACTS of KINDNESS and HELPFULLNESS, and our PATIENCE all contribute to our I~N~N~E~R BEAUTY. You see, Ladies, I~N~N~E~R is the Key Word! Because, all the makeup, hair styling products and clothing in this nation cannot compare to the beauty 'we hold inside of us', the 7 Principles proves that! When we see ourselves as a beautiful creation of GOD'S amazing artwork from the inside out, it causes people to sit up and pay attention, to ask with amazed inquisitiveness when you walk into a room. "Who is she?"

They won't be asking because your clothing is so stunning or the way you are styling your hair or the cosmetics you have displayed on your face, but because of the spirit of who you believe you are now. Your I~N~N~E~R BEAUTY is so magnetic that you draw attention! Projecting that kind of I~N~N~E~R SRENGTH should not be arrogant or egotistic; it's the healthy Self-Image that comes from the power of GOD'S Spirit-Image, HIS likeness within us! It should make us feel like shouting... "I am beautiful, because I am a MASTERPIECE of the KING of all kings, and I can accomplish all things through HIM!!!"

Yes, there's always room for improvement, but first and foremost, we need to realize and understand what all the 'junk' is that we carry around with us 24/7, in order to make changes. Our MINDS and HEARTS is where our REAL BEAUTY begins and generates from. Then, our VOICES and our ACTIONS show and tell others what we truly feel and believe about ourselves!

WHAT ABOUT OUR 'PAST' & WHAT DO WE DO WITH IT?

You ask me why GOD called someone like me to work in and create Lady's ministries, and write this book about my personal, crazy path-jumping life? Because HE knows where I've walked, HE knows the mistakes I've made, and believe me, there were mountains of them. I've asked GOD for forgiveness and HE has forgiven me of all my past sins! HE released me from the CHAINS of my PAST. And, now, HE's using my PAST to help other Ladies see that they too can have The CONFIDENCE WALK & POSTURE IN CHRIST! Ladies, HE can do the same for you and yours.

GOD gave me a passion to help other Ladies walk the roads they're on now, because I've been on a lot of the same roads, as I've just shared portions of my life with you in this book! I'm here to help any Lady who has gone through abuse from a family member, husband or any other human being, to forgive and not allow the past to have a negative influence on her present or future life. And, I'm here to share with her how she can heal from the internal scars. It was when I finally got to the point in my life that I let GOD do what HE wanted to do in my life, instead of me doing what I wanted to do in my life – that's when my life changed.

Back in 1999, I no longer wanted to live a life like I'd lived all my life, so I turned my life back over to my loving and forgiving SAVIOR and dedicated my life to HIS service and to HIS plans for me! You see, Ladies, it's never too late, GOD'S always there waiting for you.

THE SCAR OF REMINDER – GOD'S NOT FINISHED WITH ME YET!

Ladies, the rough roads I've traveled have been from some of my own choices that ended up not turning out well at all, and some came from out of my control. But, I'm still here by GOD'S grace and plan, even after my attempt of trying to take my own life when I was younger, during a rough season in a marriage during the mid '80s. My life had come to a sinking place and I didn't think I could take any more of it. Most people who know me, including family members, do not know about this. I still have the scar on my wrist to remind me that GOD wasn't finished with me yet. And, Hallelujah, HE'S still not finished! I'm so thankful my brother found me that day, before it was too late. I'm still here today, because GOD has been walking each road with me, every step of the way! Now, I'm telling my story. Ladies, one day you may feel the need to tell your story, tell of your scars – mentally and physically – of how and what GOD has helped you overcome and the healing HE has done within you. And, it could become part of someone else's survival guide, and then they will have their own story to tell... and on and on the healing and new beginnings will continue to unfold.

Psalms 119:130 tells us... 'The unfolding of our words gives light.'

⁓⧬⁓

I'm a forgiven follower of CHRIST, desiring to do HIS calling, looking forward to the rest of my future here on this earth, and also, the day I walk through the Gates of Heaven and to the days I'll be 'trying' to re-decorate heaven!

For those who don't know me, home interior decorating has always been my passion, and still is, and at different times throughout my life, has been a business of mine, so the remark about redecorating heaven is a pun. For I know Heaven will be like nothing we have ever seen with our own eyes! I'm so looking forward to seeing it and walking on the streets of gold after entering the pearly gates! **Revelation 21:21**

Ladies, when you think your past forgiven sins will keep you away from a calling that GOD has had in HIS plans all along – you're wrong. GOD uses people with all kinds of backgrounds to take the message to others who may need that special word from you, no matter what your past has been! And, remember this too... No, you do not have to be a Bible scholar to be a witness for CHRIST. I am a good example of that. I hate to admit this, but I've never been one who read or studied my Bible until later in life, so memorizing Scriptures is still a challenge for me, and my memory isn't as sharp as in the past. NO, I refuse to call myself an old woman, because I'm not, but just one whose had a lot of things get lost in this silly-crazy brain of mine!

Seriously Ladies, once you've surrendered your life over to CHRIST and surrendered to HIS calling and HIS service, HE can and will use you in so many ways. But first, you must be willing to allow HIM to do so!

Just remember this, Ladies... "NEVER walk ahead of GOD and ask HIM to follow! Instead, ask HIM to go before you to prepare the way for you, and for HIS WILL to be done in your life!"

'GOD is as a light shining in a dark place, until the day dawns and the morning star rises in your Heart.'
2 Peter 1:19b (NIV)

I finally got it! Have you got it yet?

ACTIONS WE NEED TO PUT & KEEP IN PLACE

Ladies, you have lived the PAST once already, so it's now time to...

- Ask GOD'S FORGIVENESS on your past and present sins
- NEVER REPEAT the bad – and – the – ugly past beliefs, mistakes and failures
- Ask GOD to HEAL YOU from the scars that the

PAST has left within you

- ACCEPT the HEALING as a NEW BEGINNING
- MOVE ON
- Let the scars only be a REMINDER of GOD'S HEALING, and in the spirit of HELPING SOMEONE ELSE MOVE PAST their own personal scars

ALWAYS REMEMBER THIS...

Our REAL BEAUTY comes from FOUR places within our I~N~N~E~R bodies. Do you remember those four places?

- Our MINDS
- Our HEARTS
- Our VOICES
- Our ACTIONS ... are the beliefs that are stored in the first two. Meaning... What we store in our MINDS and HEARTS will at some point come forth through our VOICES and be seen by our ACTIONS! The message... Be Extra Careful what you allow in your BRAINS to settle there because sooner or later it builds roots down into your HEARTS!

Ephesians 5:14: "WAKE UP, O SLEEPER. RISE FROM THE DEAD, AND CHRIST WILL SHINE ON YOU!"

My Motto Is... 'If you've received and learned, then you must live as an example, and help others.' So, learn to share your testimony and the knowledge/wisdom you've learned from personal trials that were given to you from your GOD through those trying times.

"THE LIVING CIRCLE"

*GOD gave from HIS Heart...
HE gave us HIS SON!
HIS SON, *JESUS, gave HIS
LIFE so that *We could receive
LIFE and Learn to Tell *Others
that they too may have LIFE.

Do You See the 'Living Circle' Here?
Where does it begin?
GOD,
JESUS,
US
and Others.

ENCOURAGEMENTS FROM THE AUTHOR

Our 911-JESUS

Beautiful Ladies, I want to thank you for reading my book and I pray that there was something within the pages that touched you in some way to draw you closer to our GOD. I pray that whatever spoke to you, you will go with GOD and use the words of statements to enrich your life from this point onward.

This was written at the beginning of this book, but always remember... We must know 'SELF' in-depth to be able to make needed changes and then we must know The CREATOR of our bodies to know... what to 'let go of' and what to 'enrich in our lives'!

People may have spoken negative things into your life, but the good news is, Ladies, people don't determine your future and where you will spend eternity, you and GOD do! Don't allow others to ruin your JOURNEY-WALK that you are walking at this moment, for they have no control over your future! Also, don't allow others to interrupt your BLESSINGS, because the 'BLESSINGS' ahead will always be greater than the battles you've left behind!

Always remember to never walk a step without JESUS by your side, learn to be a 'FOLLOWER' not someone who tells HIM "I'll see YOU when I get back"! Because, when we walk through a storm or fall into a 'pit', WHO is it that we call upon to walk with us? Our 911-JESUS! HE deserves to be recognized that HE is walking side-by-side with us at ALL TIMES.

Walking through storms in life is not where we like to see ourselves. Right? Sometimes GOD tells the STORMS to leave us alone, and then there are the times GOD tells us to leave the STORM alone. So, if at all possible, walk away from anything that you see will be causing a STORM in your life. And, for the times you can't walk away, ask GOD to go before you, and then...never let go of HIS hand!

We all have a PAST, some with great memories, some not so great. We can't change our past but we can overcome the scars that may have been left in/on us. Throughout the Chapters in this book you have learned many ways to let go of the ugly past and know you have been renewed by GOD'S cleansing blood and will no longer be held prisoner of your past. NEW

BEGINNINGS are so much more rejoiceful and rewarding than our past mistakes. 'OLD LIFE GONE and FORGIVEN but not totally forgotten, because using it as your testimony may help others to see HOPE and PEACE in their own life!'

When someone brings up your past, as in trying to remind you what sort of a person you used to be and indicating you surely can't be a Christian now, tell them 'that JESUS dropped the charges and I am now forgiven and a new creation in HIM!' Let them know they are not to judge you by your past, 'because, thank JESUS, you don't live there anymore,' and this could be a perfect opportunity to tell them about your LORD and SAVIOR! Never waste an opportunity to share what GOD has done for you and will do for others.

Take this verse to Heart in **Psalms 119:130 (NIV)... "The unfolding of YOUR words gives LIGHT; it gives understanding to the simple."**

I pray BLESSINGS to take the place of all the negatives in your life. I send my LOVE to each one who has read this book, and I say THANK YOU & may GOD BLESS YOU GREATLY!
CJ Fortson
July 10, 2020
The CONFIDENT LADY of PURPOSE MINISTRIES

I would love to hear from you on how the messages in this book has spoken to you, Feel free to share your words of rejoicing with me. My email address is...

innerbeautyconfidence@outlook.com

MY MINISTRY HISTORY...
JOURNEY WALK

OLD LIFE GONE and FORGIVEN but not totally forgotten, because using it as my testimony helps others to see HOPE and PEACE!!

My ministry actually started while I was single. After my husband died of cancer in 1996, it took me a while, but I finally turned back to Christ and surrendered my life to HIS services, and that's when the ministries began. I was honored to be the Director of our Single's Department in my home church in Lubbock, Texas. I was always available for the single Ladies to talk to when facing difficulties. I enjoyed putting together all the activities to bring our class together. Actually, at one of our fun Christmas parties in 2001 is when my husband, David, said he fell in love with me because he loved my humor! It took me a little longer to feel the same, because I was looking for those 7 Positive Things that I could respect about his character, actions/reactions and his personal 'sincere' treatments toward me and to others. It didn't take me long to see at least 7, so I fell in love with him soon afterwards!

I had never dated any man in our church nor in the Singles Class during the six years I was single. David and I had not even had any one-on-one conversations with one another, but I did know that his wife had passed away with cancer the year before. He is three years older and was so shy, but in mid-January he finally got up the courage to ask me out for coffee away from all the people in our class. GOD placed Dave in that class for more reasons than one and I'm so thankful HE did!! We married July 19, 2002 and life with my GOD-GIFT has been the greatest I've ever experienced!

Back in 2003-2004, I taught classes through what used to be ... Christian Women Job Core, and I also was blessed at becoming a mentor to one great lady who later became my personal assistant in my own Lady's Ministry. CWJC worked with Ladies from many backgrounds. Some had just come out of prison, some were just trying to get an education after dropping out of school, and others were wanting to find their way and purpose in life. I thoroughly enjoyed being a part of that nationwide ministry.

After that, I felt GOD calling me personally into a ministry that was somewhat similar to the CWJC. My ministry was called...

'The Sheltering Tree Ministries' and it was a fast growing and successful ministry from the start. The Ladies attended inspirational Bible-based Self-Help classes that we offered. The one we taught the most was from the material I wrote called... The I~N~N~E~R BEAUTY FORMULA. (This book you're reading right now was taken from that material.)

We offered a Food Pantry for our Ladies and their families who were in need. We also took donations of clothing to help provide for the Ladies who needed nice apparel when going for job interviews.

GOD blessed me with a great team and we worked closely with Ladies by confidentially mentoring those who were trying to find their way after a divorce, after losing a husband to death, those trying to recover from abusive relationships and some just wanted to find themselves and what GOD'S purpose was for their life.

I have also counseled a few Ladies who were trying to mentally and spiritually heal from having abortions. I could see their pain of carrying this guilt for years and they felt they could never recover. Initially, I wasn't sure what to say to the Ladies, but after much prayer, GOD guided me in what to say and do. The Ladies came to the point in their lives to ask GOD'S forgiveness and they believed GOD had forgiven them.

Later on, in our new church I was the leader of a Ladies' Ministry. Victory Life was a brand-new church at the time but the membership grew rapidly. We decided we needed to put in place an active Ladies' Ministry and I led that group for almost two years until my husband's job transferred him to Colorado. GOD blessed me again with some awesome Ladies who worked alongside of me in that ministry!

I have done public speaking at Christian Ladies' gatherings Becoming A Confident Lady of Purpose and that has always been a blessing to me over the years. Writing Bible Studies is a great passion of mine! I dearly love writing about the Ladies of the Bible and teaching the studies. I've written and taught more than six Bible Studies over the past years here in Texas and Colorado. Just to name a few...

- A DREAM TO REALITY', a story about Naomi's and Ruth's treacherous journey back home to Bethlehem. How they traveled through all their adversities trying to fulfill their dream to return home, and they never gave up. PART TWO isn't totally finished as of yet, it will be taught separately, and it's called... 'EMPTINESS BECOMES FULL AGAIN', this is more about Ruth and her second chance for love.
- SINGLE, SATISFIED & FULFILLED'. As you can guess this class is for the single Ladies.

- BIBLE ALIVE'. It's an in-depth study on 'how to' study the Bible.

- The I~N~N~E~R BEAUTY FORMULA' has been taught several times throughout the years and has had a profound influence on so many Ladies, to the point that GOD has laid it heavy on my Heart to share it more by publishing it as a Bible Study in a book so many more Ladies can read, understand, and experience a life of CONFIDENCE WALK and POSTURE IN CHRIST by understanding their I~N~N~E~R BEAUTY, no matter what life they have lived in the past or living at the moment.

I have written manuscripts to eventually be put into Bible studies on...

- RAHAB...'The TRUTH ABOUT RAHAB'
- HAGAR...'BEING REAL'
- 'THE LYDIAN LADY'

I've started a fiction novel from an experience I personally had on an airplane flying over the mountains of Colorado in a storm. It's called, 'Wings Under the Wing'. You can imagine what the topic of that story is all about. It's an intense story!

I'll soon be launching a new ministry that will be called... 'The Confident Lady of Purpose Ministries' so, you see, GOD isn't finished with me yet, and I say...HALLELUJAH!!!

Available for Speaking

If your church or Ladies Ministry is interested in speaking with me to be a Keynote speaker or doing a teaching retreat, please send me an email to....

innerbeautyconfidence@outlook.com

or go to my ministry FaceBook page...

The Confidence Walk & Posture In Christ Book Series

and leave me a message. Feel free to join my FB page.

"The LORD has stood at my side gave me strength, so that the message might be fully proclaimed for others to hear..." 2 Timothy 4:17

PLAN of SALVATION

The message in the BIBLE is very clear on how we can accept JESUS into our Hearts. If you are not a Christian and are ready to ask JESUS into your Heart, below are the verses in the BIBLE that will guide you to be SAVED. Read each one with an open and welcoming Heart and believe that JESUS is the SAVIOR of our souls, then ask HIM into your Heart.

- **Romans 3:23... "We have all sinned and fallen short of the glory of GOD."**
- **Romans 6:23... "For the wages of sin is death, but the GIFT of GOD is eternal life in CHRIST JESUS our LORD."**
- **John 3:16... "GOD gave HIS SON, and all who believe in HIM shall be Saved."**
- **2 Corinthians 5:21... That's why HE took on human form, taking the punishment that we deserve.**
- **Romans 5:8... "But GOD demonstrates HIS own LOVE toward us, in that while we were still sinners, CHRIST died for us."**

- **Romans 10:9-10... Asking JESUS into your Heart... "That if you confess your sins to the LORD JESUS, and believe in your Heart that GOD has raised JESUS from the dead, you shall be saved by asking HIM to come into your Heart. For with the Heart one believes unto righteousness, and with the mouth confession is made unto salvation."**
- **Romans 10:13..."For whoever calls on the name of the LORD shall be saved."**

Because of GOD's love for us, HE sent HIS SON to die in our place, taking the punishment that we deserve. GOD promises forgiveness of sins and eternal life in heaven to all who receives HIM into their Hearts. Salvation is not about certain steps we must follow to earn salvation. Yes, Christians should be baptized. Yes, Christians should publicly confess Christ as SAVIOR. Yes, Christians should turn from sin. Yes, Christians should commit their lives to obeying GOD. However, these aren't steps to salvation. They are results of salvation. Because of our sin, we cannot in any way earn salvation. Go now, and live for CHRIST and tell others of HIS LOVE and cleansing powers.

EACH ONE OF US HAVE A POSITIVE PURPOSE IN LIFE!

Have You Discovered & Explored Yours Yet?

"By the grace of GOD, I am what I am." 1 Corinthians **15:10**

THE 10 CODES OF... GETTING A HANDLE ON YOUR SOLUTIONS

1. You always have CHOICES
2. Choose Your RESPONSE – Choose Your RESULTS
3. Taking OWNERSHIP back into Your LIFE that others have stolen
4. Having the courage to know every aspect of our I~N~N~E~R personal beliefs
5. Give Yourself PERMISSION to be YOUR NEW SELF
6. Realize You may need to CHANGE Your MINDSET
7. It is a PROCESS You have to go through
8. You need to DISCOVER YOUR SIGNIFICANCE in Your Life
9. Bad Seasons of Your Life will not last forever –'SEASONS CHANGE'
10. Then move with MOVEMENT TOWARD SEEING Your DREAM BECOMING A REALITY, in order to receive the Authentic Milestone of Accomplishment Award!!!

"By the grace of GOD, I am what I am."

1 Corinthians 15:10

REFERENCES

Brandt, Andrea. "What Do We Mean By Self-Love." Dr. Andrea Brandt, PhD, MFT, March 29, 2018. https://abrandtherapy.com/what-do-we-mean-when-we-say-self-love/.

"Confidence." Dictionary.com. Dictionary.com. Accessed October 21, 2020. https://www.dictionary.com/browse/confidence.

"Motivation." Merriam-Webster. Merriam-Webster. Accessed October 21, 2020. https://www.merriam-webster.com/dictionary/motivation.

"Motivation: Definition of Motivation by Oxford Dictionary on Lexico.com Also Meaning of Motivation." Lexico Dictionaries | English. Lexico Dictionaries. Accessed October 21, 2020. https://www.lexico.com/en/definition/motivation.

"Recipe." Wikipedia. Wikimedia Foundation, September 21, 2020. https://en.wikipedia.org/wiki/Recipe.

"Self-Concept." Merriam-Webster. Merriam-Webster. Accessed October 20, 2020. https://www.merriam-webster.com/dictionary/self-concept.

"Self-Confidence." Merriam-Webster. Merriam-Webster. Accessed October 21, 2020. https://www.merriam-webster.com/dictionary/self-confidence.

"Self-Esteem." Dictionary.com. Dictionary.com. Accessed October 21, 2020. https://www.dictionary.com/browse/self-esteem.

"Self-Esteem." Merriam-Webster. Merriam-Webster. Accessed October 21, 2020. https://www.merriam-webster.com/dictionary/self-esteem.

"Self-Esteem." Wikipedia. Wikimedia Foundation, October 8, 2020. https://en.wikipedia.org/wiki/Self-esteem.

"Self-Love and What It Means." Brain & Behavior Research Foundation, July 9, 2020. https://www.bbrfoundation.org/blog/self-love-and-what-it-means.

"Self-Love." Dictionary.com. Dictionary.com. Accessed October 21, 2020. https://www.dictionary.com/browse/self-love.

"Self-Love." Merriam-Webster. Merriam-Webster. Accessed October 21, 2020. https://www.merriam-webster.com/dictionary/self-love.

"Self-Respect Definitions." YourDictionary. Accessed October 21, 2020. https://www.yourdictionary.com/self-respect.

"Self-Respect." Dictionary.com. Dictionary.com. Accessed October 21, 2020. https://www.dictionary.com/browse/self-respect?s=t.

"Self-Respect: Definition of Self-Respect by Oxford Dictionary on Lexico.com Also Meaning of Self-Respect." Lexico Dictionaries | English. Lexico Dictionaries. Accessed October 21, 2020. https://www.lexico.com/en/definition/self-respect.

"Self-Worth." Dictionary.com. Dictionary.com. Accessed October 21, 2020. https://www.dictionary.com/browse/self-worth.

"Self-Worth." Merriam-Webster. Merriam-Webster. Accessed October 21, 2020. https://www.merriam-webster.com/dictionary/self-worth.

Swindoll, Charles R. *The Grace Awakening*. Nashville: Thomas Nelson, 2003.

"Ziglar Key Influencers." Ziglar Inc, February 15, 2018. https://www.ziglar.com/why-ziglar/ziglar-key-influencers/.

CPSIA information can be obtained
at www.ICGtesting.com
Printed in the USA
LVHW021443230121
677175LV00002B/71